THE
WARRIOR
GODDESS
WAY

Also by HeatherAsh Amara

Warrior Goddess Training

Warrior Goddess Training Companion Workbook

The Toltec Path of Transformation

THE
WARRIOR
GODDESS
WAY

Claiming the Woman
You Are Destined to Be

HEATHERASH AMARA

Hierophant publishing

Cover design by Emma Smith
Cover photo by Elena Ray
Interior design by Frame25 Productions

Hierophant Publishing
8301 Broadway, Suite 219
San Antonio, TX 78209
888-800-4240
www.hierophantpublishing.com

If you are unable to order this book from your local bookseller, you may order directly from the publisher.

Library of Congress Control Number: 2016950703

ISBN: 978-1-938289-57-6

10 9 8 7 6 5 4 3 2

Printed in the USA

*For the ancestors, the ones to
come, and those embodied now.*

You never change things by fighting the existing reality.
To change something, build a new model that
makes the existing model obsolete.
—R. Buckminster Fuller

Contents

Preface

This book you are holding now is a follow-up to my previous book, the best seller *Warrior Goddess Training: Become the Woman You Are Meant to Be* (Hierophant 2014). While it's not necessary to have read that book to read this one, you may find doing so beneficial, as this book goes deeper and expands on some of the information presented in the first book. The potent Warrior Goddess Creed found on page xiv synthesizes each of the ten lessons in *Warrior Goddess Training*.

I began working with women's groups in 1987 quite by accident. After spending a mind-expanding summer reading every book in the University of California at Davis's library on earth-based spirituality and goddesses, my best friend Autumn and I decided to share what we were so passionately exploring. We hoped at least ten or so women would show up to the one-hour talk we offered on campus and were shocked when sixty women showed up instead, eager to learn about a spirituality that honored the cycles of nature and the divine feminine.

"I'll take thirty if you take thirty," Autumn said to me, and I nodded, swallowing a lump in my throat the size of a small country. I had never spoken to such a large group before, and my knees were honestly trembling. But I found I was deeply happy when I was sharing my enthusiasm for the wisdom of our female ancestors. Soon women were begging me to teach a class. I remember I charged thirteen dollars for my first eight-week series through the Experimental College at UC Davis. I've been teaching ever since, and I'm still as passionate today as I was then about sharing the most potent tools from a variety of world traditions.

Of the many teachers I've been blessed to work with, my most influential mentor was don Miguel Ruiz, author of *The Four Agreements*. His guidance, love, and vision shaped me from a young woman unsure of herself and riddled with self-judgment to the self-loving, dedicated, playful Warrior Goddess I am blessed to be today. The Toltec teachings (the Toltecs were ancient Native Americans who built the pyramids in Teotihuacan, Mexico, two thousand years ago) are a foundational part of the Warrior Goddess path, and I am deeply grateful to be part of the Ruiz family's vision of sharing Toltec wisdom in an accessible, practical, transformative way.

In my first Warrior Goddess book, *Warrior Goddess Training*, I was able to take the core of my twenty-five-plus years of apprenticeships, living, and teaching and distill it into ten lessons for helping women find their inner freedom. When I first gave the manuscript to my publisher, Randy Davila, I told him about my dream of *Warrior Goddess Training* being much more than just a book; I saw a Warrior Goddess global movement of women inspired to reclaim their full voice and power. Randy's response is what I love about working with him: "Let's do it!"

What we didn't know then was that the movement would grow beyond both of our expectations from the first day *Warrior Goddess Training* was published.

On September 4, 2014, we launched *Warrior Goddess Training* with a party and a request: I asked everyone I knew to buy a copy of the book online or at a local bookstore. That night *Warrior Goddess Training* soared to the number one bestselling spot in Shamanism and Goddesses on Amazon, which is not too unusual when you get all of your friends to buy your book on the same day. What was highly unusual was that *Warrior Goddess Training* stayed number one in those two categories day after day, month after month, year after year. And it began to show up on best seller lists in other places too: in independent bookstores, libraries, and wholesale book distributors.

And suddenly the emails started coming in from women all over the country: "I've just finished *Warrior Goddess Training* and I want to start a discussion group and share this book with all my friends. I've never done anything like this before. Any suggestions?" And so we created a Warrior Goddess book club discussion guide, and the ten lessons of the Warrior Goddess movement spread from living room to living room, circles of women coming together as their ancestors did, sharing and supporting and inspiring each other.

Next I created a Warrior Goddess facilitator training program and began teaching women how to lead their own Warrior Goddess classes. So along with the book clubs, there are now women trained to share the Warrior Goddess message as well as bring their unique flavor of the teachings to their communities.

I have tears in my eyes when I think about the many deeply personal emails I've received from women struggling with serious challenges in their life: divorce, chronic illness, children with disabilities, job loss or difficult work situations, sometimes all at the same time. Email after email, women thank me for the glimmer of hope they felt while reading *Warrior Goddess Training*, or for how the book motivated them to take action for themselves for the first time or to forgive themselves and start to really listen to and follow their inner needs and desires. Women already on a spiritual/healing path found life-changing tools in *Warrior Goddess Training* that they hadn't found in their years of study and practice. At workshops, I often hear women say, "I never knew I could feel this supported and seen and inspired by a group of women I just met!" We may start as strangers, but with the new language we are creating with the Warrior Goddess principles, we become a family, we become a tribe (and if we are going to transform ourselves and the world, we need a conscious, kick-ass, Warrior Goddess tribe!).

After witnessing the healing ripple of *Warrior Goddess Training* and seeing women rise to the Warrior Goddess call to action—to shed the old layers of who they think they are supposed to be to become the women they are meant to be—I feel even more dedicated to supporting women's inner liberation. My passion is to bring practical, step-by-step guidance to women, not just intellectual theory or feel-good words. Imagining what we would like to be different and looking at beautiful quotes and pictures on Facebook are not enough. In order to make change, we must act. And in order to act to make change, we must stop trying to "fix ourselves" using judgment, comparison, fear, blame, and self-punishment.

We are not broken, or helpless, or beyond redemption. Within each one of us, regardless of our outer circumstances, is a sacred spark that craves to be rekindled and stoked back to a sustained, wild, fiery blaze; an ancestral wisdom deep in the marrow of our bones and in the very fabric of our DNA that yearns to be touched and awakened. It is time to let go of striving to be perfect, looking outside of ourselves for answers, and waiting for something or someone else to save, fix, or transform us. It is time to release the heaviness of taking care of everyone else and putting ourselves last, time to stop being our worst enemy, time to stop putting our dreams on hold.

It is time to continue the inner revolution.

Warrior Goddess, I hold out my hand to walk with you through the old layers of hurt, shame, stuckness, and self-criticism.

Welcome to the Warrior Goddess tribe.

Warrior Goddess Creed

This creed is derived from the ten lessons in *Warrior Goddess Training*. As you enter the realm of *The Warrior Goddess Way*, I invite you to read the Warrior Goddess Creed out loud, as doing so is an outward expression of your inner commitment to be the real you.

I hereby commit to fully embody my Warrior Goddess self.
From this moment forward, I will do my best to:

Love all of my being

Appreciate the beginnings and the endings

Honor my body and mind as a temple

Stay grounded and present

Cultivate my passions and creativity

Own my strength and vulnerability

Open my heart to all of life

Speak my deepest truths

Listen to the wisdom within

Claim my unique path

And walk the Warrior Goddess Way.

Introduction

As you will see in the pages that follow, the Warrior Goddess Way is not a path to instant self-love, enlightenment, or happiness (though all these things could happen in an instant). Nor is it a method to finally finding the partner of your dreams, having the perfect job, or being the perfect specimen of health and vitality (though all of these things could happen to you too).

The Warrior Goddess Way is a pathway of presence, baby steps, and practice. It is a road to reclaiming all of you—your darkest fears and your most precious gifts. The Warrior Goddess Way invites you to bring your compassion, love, and humor to the entirety of your being on your walk to becoming the woman you are meant to be. This is a core rewiring of how you have been trained as a woman, a digging up of the old foundation to replace it, brick by brick, with a new, more solid and resilient structure.

For too many of us, the floor we've built our life on is made up of wobbly blocks of self-judgment, comparison, caretaking, and valuing everyone else's needs before our own. This cracked foundation never allows us to rest into the peacefully joyful and fiery, creative women we are at our essence. Instead, we spend our time with a destabilizing sense (either whispered or shouted) of not being good enough, not being able to do it "right," and an abiding need to be liked and approved of.

The Warrior Goddess Way is about changing this paradigm.

Shortly after *Warrior Goddess Training* was published, I began holding Warrior Goddess Wisdom Weekend gatherings as a way to go deeper into the teachings and allow women from all over the world to connect with one another in person. The women who came to these events were hungry to make connections with one another, as many had been unable to share certain aspects of themselves with those in their everyday lives. They yearned for the healing power of community, and the Warrior Goddess Wisdom Weekend events were designed to provide exactly that.

So many women I've worked with feel isolated and alone, cut off from other women for support, comfort, and encouragement (even in a world that is more "connected" than ever before). I should also point out that this is a relatively modern phenomenon. In ancient tribal cultures, women worked side by side, singing, talking, and praying as they did. Grinding corn, digging for roots, and making clothes were not considered individual activities; their labor was a community gathering that brought celebration and connection. Even though the work was sometimes hard and often repetitive, our grandmothers' grandmothers knew they were part of a greater whole that nourished everyone. And so the work was done in joy, mutual support, and a deep sense of belonging.

As you read *The Warrior Goddess Way*, I invite you to consider yourself part of a global tribe of women working together to heal the old collective wounds of the feminine. You are not just doing this inner work for yourself, but for all women. And for all children, alive and still unborn. And for all men, so we may inspire, support, and insist with love that they do their inner work. And for the planet, our Mother who needs her daughters whole and clear. The truth is that we heal the world by healing ourselves.

I invite you to put down the burdens of trying to fix others and the distractions of comparison and judgment. I invite you to show up as you, for you, knowing that you are every woman. Your devotion to your path is at its core your devotion to all that you love. Make this commitment to yourself, and as you do, feel the web of your Warrior Goddess sisters, working beside you, for the greater good of all. Feel your willingness, courage, tenacity, resilience. You've come this far; let's continue this walk of transformation together.

And don't forget: everything is conspiring to help you claim the woman you are destined to be. What you often label as roadblocks in your life are actually doorways to discovering deeper truths about yourself, because it's often the unplanned or unwanted situations in your life that show you the immense reservoir of strength that resides at the core of your being. May the words contained in this book inspire you to ask yourself the important questions, support you in listening deeply for the answers, and entice you to take new actions to reclaim your joyful, creative, and divine essence.

As for me, before I began doing this inner work I could easily be described as someone who was highly self-judgmental. I constantly worried about what other people thought of me, and, to round things off, I also expected nothing less than perfection from myself in all areas. As you can imagine, this was not a formula for a content and joyful existence.

To make matters worse, instead of attending to my mind and questioning these self-limiting thoughts, I let them run rampant, like a little kid after way too much sugar. Instead of getting to know who I really was, I fussed about who I wasn't. Instead of inhabiting my body, I thought about my body and why it wasn't tall enough, short enough, skinny enough, or whatever other "enough" I thought I needed to be for myself on that particular day.

Fortunately, I can tell you that this is not how my life is today. That's because after incorporating the ten lessons of *Warrior Goddess Training* into my life, I discovered three additional principles that have guided me further down the path to inner freedom: Wisdom, Authenticity, and Yes! These three principles have helped me become the woman that I am today, and they are the foundation of the Warrior Goddess Way. As you will see in the pages that follow, life is much like the proverbial onion: there are always more translucent, closer-to-the-core layers to peel back.

The good news is that as a result of implementing these three tools into my life, the majority of the time I am highly self-amused, I am clear about who I am and what I want, and I actually enjoy making mistakes and learning from them. I say the majority of the time because there are still moments when I melt down fabulously, get overcome with fear and doubt, or become consumed by what people think of me. But I can tell you that these are *moments* rather than days or extended periods of time, and compared to how I was once, these moments are extremely rare.

You see, the truths I will outline here, the ones that ultimately became the Warrior Goddess Way, were not the result of an overnight one-shot fix, but rather a twenty-five year process of unfolding. There was no cataclysmic event that occurred in my life—no near-death experience, no beings from other galaxies wanting to be channeled through me to reveal the wisdom of the spirit realm, and I wasn't struck by lightning. As I look back, I can see that my inner Warrior Goddess bubbled forth gradually, like a spring that rises to the surface once the good, strong rains follow a long drought.

I can also see that the potential for awakening was always there. Good guidance from my many dear teachers and friends and some very overworked guardian angels, along with my dogged persistence, laid the foundation for blossom after blossom to unfurl from a once parched landscape. Today, I can honestly say that my spiritual path weaves through and interpenetrates every part of my life. Scrubbing the bathroom floor and communing with God are not separate. People sometimes marvel at how I can fluidly switch between washing dishes, teaching, hanging out with friends, and doing my taxes. It is because, from the Warrior Goddess perspective, they are all ways to connect with the Divine. Yes, even the taxes.

I actually get excited when it is time to figure out our taxes. And go to the dentist. And when I have to answer a difficult email. I'm not a masochist; I just love to enjoy and be fully present with everything. And when I am not enjoying something, I am aware of that and curious about it. How can I be more present with this? What do I need to shift? Sometimes I can shift it immediately; sometimes it takes me a few years. It's all good.

And here is the best part: I am no different from you. You CAN love to enjoy everything too. Your potential for dancing rather than dragging through life is also waiting to be reawakened. It doesn't matter how horrible your childhood was, how bad your ex hurt you, or even how miserable you think your life is now. Your inner Warrior Goddess is waiting patiently, ready to be freed from your inner tyranny.

You just need to come home . . . to yourself.

That's the path of the Warrior Goddess, and it really is the one less traveled. *The Warrior Goddess Way* is a road map for coming back home to yourself. Fully. How I see the transformation is this: in the old way of being each of us has a physical body, but we live outside of ourselves, putting all our attention on the image of perfection that lives in our minds only. We constantly look to this "perfect" woman we believe we are supposed to be to see where we are not doing it right, where we are falling short, where we should have said or done something else. Instead of living from our center, we relentlessly compare ourselves to this illusion.

In the new way of being we bring all of our compassion, wisdom, presence, and play back into this place and this time. We come back home. We learn to see through our eyes, sense with all of our senses, and stay in this moment with the being that we are. Coming home to ourselves, we suddenly have the power to heal and transform. First ourselves, and then in a widening spiral to all those around us.

Wisdom arises naturally when we learn to listen. Not to the voices in our head, but the voices in our cells. Not to our internal judge, but to our natural discernment. Not to our disaster mind, but to our creative knowing. Everything you need is within. The Warrior Goddess Way will help you come home to your wise woman self.

Authenticity is not something to strive for on the outside; it is something to embrace from the inside. You don't become authentic by being right or good or spiritual. You become authentic by embracing your vulnerability, your silliness, and owning all your superpowers. You become authentic when you accept and love where you are in the moment, especially in those times that whatever you are experiencing doesn't match the image of what you think "should be." The Warrior Goddess Way shows you how to walk the path of embodied you-ness.

And *Yes!* is about celebrating. Everything. All the time. And that is one serious art not for the faint of heart. Most of us love to celebrate our successes, but what I'm talking about is celebrating even your greatest defeats. This means looking for the gift in every situation, even when something doesn't go your way. Finding joy in your grief. Enthusiastically embracing your shadow. High-fiving yourself when you screw up, and then bringing 100 percent of yourself to the next action.

The good news is that not only have I experienced a profound shift in my own life though practicing these tools, I have witnessed a shift in many others who have traveled the same path. I have a friend and student who has struggled mightily with serious childhood mental, emotional, and sexual abuse. The trauma she experienced early in life weighed heavily on her for years. But after spending time doing this inner work, I am pleased to say that things have changed for her, and it started with a shift in her perception. By being inspired to bring her attention fully to what she needed, she finally started the journey of coming home to herself. Suddenly, the prospect of looking squarely at the abuse she suffered was not a frightening nightmare to be avoided at all costs, but an exciting pathway to transforming her relationship with herself. Because she is walking this path, she is now open to a new world of possibilities. This type of profound shift in thinking and being is what I want for you.

How to Use This Book

I have organized this book into three parts to reflect the three pillars of the Warrior Goddess Way: Wisdom, Authenticity, and Yes! Each chapter contains nutritious, easily digestible, bite-size nuggets of playful practicality. We will explore topics such as forgiveness, respect, and stillness. We will uncover and release your blocks, stuck places, and repetitive habits. We will delve into cleaning, relationships, communication, and the power of conscious beginnings and endings.

Each chapter also contains some practices to help you to integrate the Warrior Goddess Way into the marrow of your bones. You can do one of the practices a week, or one a day, or never do any of them, ever. But remember, each practice is an excellent bridge for taking the black-and-white pages from this book into the colorful fullness of your life. You get to explore how to best integrate what you learn.

Throughout these teachings and exercises I will also share with you one woman's journey to embodying her strength, integrity, and grace while embracing her bouts of shyness, gawkiness, and endless capacity to get lost while driving.

Let us begin the Warrior Goddess Way.

Part One

WISDOM

Wisdom arises naturally when we learn to listen. Not to the voices in our head, but the voices in our cells. Not to our internal judge, but to our natural discernment. Not to our disaster mind, but to our creative knowing. Everything you need is within. *The Warrior Goddess Way* will help you come home to your wise woman self.

When you are in touch with wisdom, you are able to spot and release all the places of comparison, judgment, and worry; all the hard edges of trying to be perfect, trying to do it right, trying to be loved; and all the stuck places where you live in the past or project into the future, consumed by thinking, wanting to figure everything out, trying to understand.

When you release these things through the power of wisdom, what does that leave you with? The truth of the woman you are destined to be—without apology, need to justify, or need to diminish. You will come back home to your natural state of wonder, curiosity, and awe. You will play. You will see the perfection of yourself and others, flaws and all.

As you go deeper into your wisdom, you will uncover layer upon layer of stories, old emotions, and patterns of holding on to things that no longer serve you. Sometimes you will need to bring in the heat of fire to burn away the old, sometimes the softness of water to gently cleanse. Sometimes warrior fierceness, sometimes goddess compassion. Your wisdom will show you which tool is needed for each situation.

ONE

The Wisdom of Presence

Common sense dictates that we evaluate our beliefs
on the basis of how they affect us. If they make us
more loving, creative, and wise, they are good beliefs.
If they make us cruel, jealous, depressed, and sick,
they cannot be good beliefs or memes.
—Barbara Marx Hubbard

The center point of the Warrior Goddess Way stems from an invaluable inner treasure: a conscious commitment to loving and respecting your beautiful self, without conditions or exceptions. Here is where you make a stand, saying to all of creation: "I am willing to show up for myself 100 percent, in this moment, in this place. I mark my intent to stand firm in the present, to release both the regret of the past and any fear of the future, and to honor what is true and best for me in the Now."

I have found again and again that we have to relinquish hoping, wishing, and wanting things to be different in order to show up for ourselves fully. This end to wanting things to be different can be transformed into a commitment to love yourself for who you are, without judgment, comparison, or avoidance. This is the Warrior Goddess Way. When you can say, "This is who I am now" from a place of presence and loving assessment, you reclaim your power to choose who you want to be and who you want to become.

It seems like a bit of a paradox to say, "To change who I am, I begin by accepting myself for who I am now." Most of us have worked from the self-rejection model of transformation, which says, "To change who I am, I need to punish myself for who I am now."

Take a moment to notice the energetic difference between these two statements. Say them out loud one at a time, and then close your eyes and notice how they resonate inside of you.

"To change who I am, I need to punish myself for who I am now."

"To change who I am, I begin by accepting myself for who I am now."

What do you feel when you speak each of these sentences aloud? For me, when I say that I need to punish myself for who I am now, it's as if I can feel my body contract, and a sense of hopelessness overwhelms me; but when I make the statement that change begins with acceptance, it's as if a deep, relaxing energy envelops me.

It's understandable why so many of us adopted the "self-rejection is necessary to change" model. If you look around the world today, the flawed idea that change begins with self-punishment is presented as fact in many instances. This is especially true for women, who are ridiculed if their bodies don't look a certain way (social media has provided the latest outlet for this type of misogynist behavior) or if they behave in a manner that is considered "unladylike."

The messages we receive as women are impossible to live up to. Be nice. Be bold. Be sexy. Be virginal. Take care of everyone else; you are not important. Be supermom. Be everything your partner wants you to be. Be yourself, but don't be selfish. Don't rock the boat. Don't offend others. Hide your femininity or you'll be harassed. Be feminine or you are not really a woman. All that matters is how you look. Based on these deprecating and contradictory messages, it's no wonder so many of us begin to self-scold because we feel we are not enough or we are not doing it "right."

As a result, bringing total and complete acceptance of where you are *right now* can be one of the most difficult changes to make. But the difference you will feel when you live your life accordingly is radical. Acceptance gently opens the door of creative healing and possibility, whereas punishment closes the door with an angry slam.

I should know, because I used to slam internal doors a lot. I acted more like a resentful drill sergeant than a loving friend to myself. The harsh commands of "you should," "you must," and "you have to" echoed through my mind as I struggled to keep up what I thought it meant to be a "good girl."

This desire to be seen as "good" that plagues so many women often starts when we are very young. At seven years old I remember posing for a photograph and trying to arrange myself so I would be seen as a good girl, which in my mind meant quiet, sweet, small, and pleasing to others. I have no idea where I picked these thoughts up—probably from fairy tales and TV shows and the invisible threads of agreements handed down silently through the experiences of my female ancestors. I didn't want to be myself. I wanted to be the little girl everyone loves all the time. And so I developed a habit of trying and failing to live up to an impossible standard, which meant I was disappointed in myself all the time.

But after years of living from this place of self-judgment and self-punishment, I noticed that nothing really changed in my life. I kept ending up in the same situations, relationships, and drama, and I didn't feel happy or fulfilled much of the time. This suffering brought me to an epiphany: *real and lasting change cannot be accomplished via self-punishment.* And it was when I experienced this realization that I looked my inner drill sergeant in the eye and handed in my resignation. I was ready to trust that there was a better way to grow than through self-pummeling. In that moment, I made an inner commitment to show up for myself with gratitude and love, rather than with judgment, punishment, and the inner anguish and frustration that accompanies this self-berating habit.

Showing up for yourself begins with letting go of being "good" or "perfect" and accepting where you are now, wherever that happens to be. And this is something that I can tell you from personal experience is much easier said than done. Most of us do pretty well when it comes to accepting the things we like about ourselves, but this changes pretty quickly when it comes to the things we don't like. In my own case, it took more time and inner work to fully befriend myself and to learn to witness rather than to scold myself when I come across areas where I want to make changes. That being said, I can affirm that it was worth all the time and hard labor to uncover and give myself the gift of self-love.

Self-love can sometimes be confused with narcissism or self-centered egotism, so let me take a moment to further define what I mean by this term. Self-love is an action, and you practice it every time you look within yourself, listen to your heart, and honor what you hear. This does not mean you don't give care or concern to the feelings and opinions of others, but it has been my experience that most women don't have a problem in the area of being considerate of others. The problem is that many women I know have a tendency to go too far in that direction, putting the needs of others ahead of their own, and when we do this, we aren't being considerate of ourselves. Self-love is what allows you to bring balance to your life and your world. You honor your own needs, desires, and choices, giving them at least as much attention as you would those who are close to you.

When Do You Reject and Punish Yourself?

Self-love and self-rejection can't occupy the same space at the same time, so showing up for and loving yourself in every moment means identifying, acknowledging, and releasing the areas that you are still subtly (or not so subtly) beating yourself up for. As you learn to spot and release these negative thoughts the moment they arise, your life becomes immensely more enjoyable, as you are no longer inhibited by false beliefs about what it means to be the real you.

In *Warrior Goddess Training*, I covered many of the overt ways in which we reject and punish ourselves—for instance, when we look in the mirror and criticize ourselves for what we see, or when we try so hard to make another person happy at our own expense, or when an intimate relationship ends and we judge ourselves as being undesirable, flawed, or even unlovable.

Even after we are firmly planted on the Warrior Goddess path, these harsh voices can still come up from time to time. But they are also easier to recognize. This doesn't mean they are easy to release, but they are often the judgments that we deal with first once we begin this inner work, because they scream the loudest.

In addition to spotting and releasing your severest judgments, the Warrior Goddess Way is about going deeper, seeing the judgments that, although subtler, can be just as harmful to your inner peace. Like when you punish yourself for making a simple mistake, or internally compare yourself to someone else and then judge yourself as inadequate (or superior, which is actually a setup for feeling inadequate in the future). As Sophie recently wrote me,

> I've been working toward being more compassion-ate and patient with myself. For a small mistake, eating that extra cookie, or forgetting someone's name, I can just get so hard on myself and scold myself internally—until I catch myself, take a step back, reevaluate the situation and the severity of the perceived offense, and calm myself down.

Another one of my students, I'll call her Tanya, has strug-gled with that subtle but nagging belief that she is not beauti-ful enough, feminine enough, or smart enough to be loved by another in a deeply intimate way. She turned to drugs and alcohol and food addiction when she was young to drown out these voices, which of course did not work and only created more self-hatred. After years of recovery, she realized that she may have stopped the external addictions, but her addiction to comparing herself to other women and binging on self-criticism was running rampant. One day she showed up for class beaming and literally jumping up and down.

> HeatherAsh, I finally understand what you have been saying! I have to accept myself first. I've spent my whole life feeling rejected and believing that I was so flawed as a woman no one could even look at

me, much less love me. But that was all me rejecting myself. Yesterday I looked in the mirror and started to judge myself and I was able to stop and just say hello! I accepted this is the body I have, and I chose to love it rather than hate it. I know I still have a ways to go, but this is a new era!

If we are unaware, all the little ways in which we don't accept ourselves can act like the low hum of a refrigerator, continuously buzzing in the background but rarely, if ever, noticed. It is only when we turn to face the noise of our inner negative buzz with compassion and presence that we can see and finally spot and release the damage that we are doing to ourselves, day in and day out.

As women, many of our subtle self-judgments can also be related to the quest for perfectionism, as the messages we hear in society encourage us to be the perfect wife, daughter, friend, boss, mom. The image of perfection for a woman used to be wearing pearls and heels while vacuuming the house and having dinner on the table and a big smile when her kids and husband came home. The modern image of perfection for a woman now involves having a fulfilling and interesting career, being a great soccer mom who does everything for her kids, and doing yoga four days a week in her spare time. The standards we hold ourselves and each other to are so high they make us believe we are never good enough, no matter how much we are doing.

It's interesting that most women I know will readily shake their heads in agreement with the statements "no one's perfect" or "we all make mistakes," yet when it comes to ourselves we have difficulty applying this eternal truth.

And yes, I am writing from personal experience, as I catch myself doing this very thing. Anytime I notice myself utter any variation of the word *should*, either out loud or in my head, that's my cue to pay close attention to my thoughts, because I am often not accepting who and where I am in the present moment, but instead scolding myself for not being the way I think I "should" be. Present moment acceptance, in each and every moment, is the first step in showing up for yourself. Learning to spot, identify, and release any ways in which you are subtly self-judging or self-punishing is the key to this acceptance. As I explored my "shoulds," I also noticed that at times instead of using the word *should* I was using its close cousins, *if* and *would*, because these subtly helped me create a list of conditions that I felt I needed to live up to at all times. Then, I would internally punish myself for not doing so.

In this way, I was making the positive practices and transformative tools of being a Warrior Goddess into whips that could be used for self-scolding. Here are some examples of what I caught myself thinking:

- If I were a good Warrior Goddess, I would be loving and peaceful all the time.

- As a good Warrior Goddess, I should never get triggered and react emotionally.

- If I were a good Warrior Goddess, I would never be afraid.

Consequently, when moments arose where I felt afraid of what people thought of me, got triggered and reacted emotionally, or otherwise behaved less than loving and peaceful at all times, I would begin to beat myself up internally. One day I caught myself doing this, and it suddenly occurred to me that I had transformed the Warrior Goddess principles into tools to self-flagellate. Oh, the irony of it all!

Of course, I know from talking with others that I am not alone. Many women I have worked with have consciously or unconsciously created a list of perfections that is based on what's important to them as individuals. Think about your own life for a moment. Do you have a list of perfect ideals you try to live up to? Perhaps it's a list of Warrior Goddess perfections like mine, or maybe you can relate to some of the examples from women I have worked with:

- If I were a good mother, I would never lose my temper with my children.

- If I were a good boss/employee/coworker, I would never miss a goal or deadline.

- If I were a good wife or partner, I would always be able to make my partner happy.

- If I were a good woman, I wouldn't weigh as much as I do.

- If I were a good friend, I'd always be available.

- If I were a good daughter, I would let my mom live with us even though we don't get along at all.

- If I were a good female, I would always be attractive and pleasing.

- If I were a good Warrior Goddess, I'd be a lot more courageous.

- As a single mother, I should be strong enough to meet all my kids' needs for both myself and their father.

- If I were a worthy partner, I should be able to find a compatible mate.

Take a moment to make a list of your perfection ideals and how you judge yourself when you fall short of them. Notice how beliefs such as these set the stage for the old model of "To change who I am, I need to punish myself for who I am now."

Next, I want you to say this statement out loud: "No one is perfect, including me!" Feel the energy of self-love and self-acceptance when you do so. You can also say, "Everyone is perfect, including me!" because in truth these statements are saying the same thing, as we are all perfectly imperfect. Both statements acknowledge the same truth from different perspectives, like when two people see the same event from opposite sides of the room. Both are true, depending on how you look at them. Which one feels better to you?

The belief that "self-punishment is necessary to change" is so strong that it takes a lot of Warrior Goddess concentration to notice all the ways in which you self-judge or otherwise hold yourself to an impossible standard. We will come back to this a little later in this chapter (and look at how to rewrite your list!), but first let's take a deeper look at the apparatus that makes all of these judgments possible.

The Mind and You

Have you ever noticed that the only place you experience a self-judgment, self-punishment, and any other lack of self-love is in your mind? In other words, your nose does not judge you, your thighs do not judge you, and your hips don't judge you either. On the contrary, your entire body is supporting you, even when you treat it unkindly. In this way, it's more accurate to say that your body loves you unconditionally.

But that's not the case for your mind, is it?

All of your judgments are thoughts, nothing more. So the problem isn't in your body; it's in your thinking. While the distinction that your mind is the only place that judgment can arise may seem fairly obvious, the implications of realizing this are often overlooked. That's because the thinking mind is held in such high regard in our culture that many of us associate who we really are with the mind rather than contemplating the true immensity of ourselves, of which the mind is just a part.

Many ancient cultures and wisdom traditions understood this, and that's why they use the heart as the physical placeholder where the real you resides rather than the mind. Of course, even the heart is just a metaphor, but it does serve as a good substitute or "re-minder" that the real you is so much more than the mind can understand.

The reality is that your mind is not the entire you, but only a part of you. Despite its insistence to the contrary, your mind cannot contain, describe, or fully understand who you are at the deepest level. Your mind has only a teeny, tiny, itsy-bitsy grasp of one aspect of who you are. And not only that, it doesn't do a very good job of describing you accurately, *since it often thinks you should be something else*. In this way, it's like the mind has a huge handicap, because it cannot understand the totality of you.

When we get caught up in the busyness of our lives, we can easily start to believe that we are just our thoughts being carried around by a body. But you are so much more than your thoughts, or your body. The real you is a perfect blend of spirit and matter, a sacred dance of energy embodied in form. Imagine clearing away the need to understand, label, and control everything around you. That's what the mind likes to do, but your real self doesn't cling to these mind tools. Your real self, who you are at the deepest level, is a pure force of nature, expressed through form, and an amazing, crazy-cool, utterly unique creation of brilliant perfection. Really.

Imagine shedding the need to be right or perfect or anything at all. Imagine looking at the world through the delighted eyes of a child and the quiet wisdom of an elder. Imagine your heart taking the lead and loving all manifestations of experience. When you experience these moments, you touch the real you, the one that can become buried under mind layers of past and future thinking, the endless habit of categorizing people, places, and things, and especially yourself, into good or bad, right or wrong, okay or damaged.

To be sure, the mind is a wonderful tool when tamed, but it can also be a huge block to inner peace when it runs the show. You can spend years in meditation or doing practices to quiet your mind, but if you don't spot and release the mind's habitual judgments—or the distorted perceptions of who it thinks you *should* be—not much will change. Meditation and other calming practices can help your mind relax, but underneath this calmer self will remain a sense of unworthiness and unease.

The good news is that it's been my experience that as you begin to recognize and release the ways in which you judge and punish yourself, you can simultaneously retrain your mind to view the internal self as a magical, multidimensional, magnificent self, rather than one that is not enough, broken, or that often alternates between thinking you are better than others or worse than others, depending on its mood. Doing so involves the process of learning to love yourself in all your manifestations. Love the scared "me" and the on-top-of-the-world "me" and the I-just-made-a-huge-mistake "me" and the I-just-attained-my-goal "me."

At the most basic level, a judgment is simply the mind labeling some things as "good" and other things as "bad." This is a habit of the mind that most of us have adopted. The Warrior Goddess Way is about rewiring the mind and removing the ideas of "good" and "bad" from your thinking when it comes to understanding yourself. In other words, it's time to stop trying to be good, or enough, or perfect, and just be. And you're never bad. It's just that sometimes we all do things that in retrospect we can see didn't evolve us, or didn't produce the desired outcome. This is how we learn, and as the wonderful woman Maya Angelou wrote, "When you know better, you do better."

As we walk further down the path of the Warrior Goddess Way, I invite you to take a different approach to dealing with your mind. When the mind begins to judge you, or label you as either good or bad, or criticize and scold you, rather than take it so seriously, learn to say, "Oh, there's my mind, doing what it does!" Eventually, you may even laugh at yourself when you hear your mind tell you to try to live up to an impossible way of being!

This is the new habit of self-love. And once you've practiced it, you really do become your own best friend, your own fairy godmother, warrior, guru, and goddess all rolled into one luscious package with one destiny: to rescue your precious heart from the judgments of your mind. And the good news is that you already have everything you need to celebrate exactly who you are and to creatively cultivate (not force or judge or pine for) who you would like to be. Once we fully accept and love ourselves, we realize that everywhere is home. And by owning the uniqueness of our one, we realize we are the many. This is authentic wisdom celebrating itself.

Rewriting the Judgments, Retraining the Mind

Now let's go back to the lists we made a little earlier in this chapter, but with the intent of retraining your mind to love and accept every aspect of you, including the areas where you self-judge or hold yourself to an unattainable standard. I invite you to rewrite the list you created earlier, and as you do so, lean into this statement: "To change, I must first accept where I am right now." Feel the energy of self-love and self-acceptance as you begin to rewrite that list. Below are my rewrites:

- As a Warrior Goddess, I sometimes make spectacular mistakes, and I trust that everything happens for a reason.

- As a Warrior Goddess, I sometimes react emotionally, and I am learning to be more loving toward myself and others.

- As a Warrior Goddess, I sometimes get triggered, and I use these times to learn more about myself and my agreements.

- As a Warrior Goddess, I sometimes feel afraid, and I'm learning to hold myself with compassion and love through my fears.

Now it's your turn. Take the lists that you wrote earlier and rewrite them. Do so from a place that acknowledges you have ideals you would like to live up to, but that sometimes this won't happen, because that's the reality of it, and that's okay. This is unconditional self-love in action. It's a wonderful practice to set goals and strive to do better in certain areas, but doing so from a place of self-love means that you do so without self-punishment.

Once you have made your new list, write your name at the top with the words "Personal Creed" next to it. I invite you to recite the Warrior Goddess Creed found in the introduction of this book every day, and then follow it up with your own personal creed (what you just wrote) for the next two weeks. This will help you to step into your life present, aware, and in the Warrior Goddess Way, and honor the truth of who you really are.

Wisdom: Presence Resources

Gifts

- Consciously commit to loving and respecting your beautiful self without conditions or exceptions.

- Beware of the subtle self-sabotage of using the words *should*, *if*, and *would*.

- Remember that your mind is a wonderful tool, but it needs serious training away from judgment and toward acceptance.

Explorations

The mind is constantly judging everything it sees (including ourselves) and then telling stories about it. We will take

a deeper look at these stories in the next chapter. But before
we move on, let's do an exercise that can take you out of your
mind and help you connect with the immensity that you are.

AWARENESS EXPLORATION:
YOU ARE NOT JUST YOUR MIND

Read the following exercise over a few times, then put the
book down and do the exercise as best you can from memory.
Remember, you don't have to do this perfectly.

Start by getting comfortable and taking a few breaths
into your belly. Relax your shoulders and keep your belly soft.
Close your eyes.

Bring your awareness to your big toe. Take a few breaths
into your toe, sensing your big toe and how it feels. Notice its
relation to your shoe or sock or the air. Pay attention to how
your toe is connected to your foot. Then move your awareness
to the palm of one hand. Breathe into your palm, noticing
textures and sensations and temperature.

Now bring your awareness to three other areas in your
body, using your breath to drop into the sensations of each
spot. You can pick anywhere: throat, top of your head, sacrum,
behind your knees, your right ear. The intent is to move your
attention from thinking into feeling.

Once you sense that your mind has slowed down a bit,
start recalling times in your life when you acted from your
heart or your knowing, without your mind needing to understand or comment. It might be a time you were walking and
enjoying the birdsong and colors, or were immersed in a creative project, had a strong intuitive knowing, or felt love and
gratitude for a child, friend, or beloved. Practice resting into
this feeling of connection and notice how you perceive it in

your body. Spend as much time here as possible. If you notice yourself thinking, gently bring yourself back to the feeling sense you are exploring.

When you are ready, open your eyes and look around the room, doing your best to not label or categorize anything around you. Imagine you have never seen any of the things around you before. How would you take them in, not from your mind but from your being? What is the difference between how your mind perceives things and how you experience the world around you without the mind and its stories?

NOTICE AND RELEASE THE SELF-JUDGMENTS

Showing up for yourself 100 percent of the time begins with spotting and releasing all the areas where you self-judge, subtly and not so subtly. Think back over the past few weeks (or the past few hours) and make a list of any areas where you have self-judged or self-punished, or think about the areas where you try to be perfect. These can certainly include the overt examples we covered in *Warrior Goddess Training*, as they likely still come up from time to time, but I'd also like you to notice any sneaky ways you self-judge and self-punish, as these are often more difficult to catch. Here is my list:

- I got lost driving to an appointment and was late.
  I scolded myself for being bad with directions, not leaving earlier, and making others wait.

- I set a goal to do yoga and then got involved in something else. I beat myself up for not following through.

- I missed a deadline for a project at work and internally berated myself for doing so.

- I was meditating with a group and forgot to turn my phone off. It rang, and I scolded myself for leaving it on.

Now it's time to rewrite them! Doing so is practice for retraining your mind. As I've gotten better at this over the years, I've begun to replace those thoughts of self-rejection with ones of self-love and self-acceptance. Here are my rewrites:

- I am learning discipline and the power of being on time, but there are times when I will run late.

- I commit to doing yoga once or twice a week and supporting myself in my practice, and sometimes I will miss a session.

- I do my best to meet deadlines at work, but this won't always happen, and that's okay.

- I am considerate of others and usually remember to turn my phone off when I meditate, except when I forget to.

Now it's your turn. Rewrite your list while leaning into the statement, "To change who I am, I begin by accepting myself for who I am now."

TWO

The Wisdom of Stories

Turn your wounds into wisdom.
—Oprah Winfrey

In the last chapter, we looked at the mind's judgments, or the areas that the mind subtly (or not so subtly) thinks should be different or perfect. When these self-judgments go unnoticed, they ultimately get strung together to make entire stories, and before you know it, you are writing a novel within yourself that is based on self-rejection, self-punishment, or otherwise failing to meet some imaginary image of perfection.

These stories create a personal narrative of who we think we are and how we express ourselves in the world, and our minds are the consummate storytellers. But when we realize that our mind's perspective is skewed, and that the mind is simply a *part* of us rather than the entirety of us, we can begin to see the stories it tells as just that—simply stories. And we have the power to change those stories.

We can bring unconditional love and compassion to our stories and ourselves, and this allows space for our stories to be transformed. A story is dependent on its storyteller, and when we realize this we can shift our perspective and rewrite our stories, making them a part of our conscious creation, dynamic and beautiful, regardless of the events of our past.

Rewriting our stories is the difference between living a life that is based on the programming that we adopted from the world we grew up in versus living from a place of true power and inspiration, where we are the heroine of our stories rather than the victim. One way is unconscious, where you are trapped by circumstances, and the latter is the Warrior Goddess Way, where you realize the story is dependent upon you, not the other way around. You can transcend your inherited stories and replace them with literally whatever you want. You potential, your possibility, is infinite.

I believe that we are here, as women, to radically shift our perspective to release our stories of fear and self-doubt and consciously create a new story that is grounded in presence and self-fulfillment. This is the wisdom of the story in action, and it is the key to transforming your world.

In *Warrior Goddess Training*, I shared a story I used to tell myself, and anyone who asked me, about my difficult childhood. I realized one day that every time I shared my story it made me feel depleted, sorry for myself, and helpless. Here is a summary of that story:

> I was traumatized as a child by how often my family moved. I went to eight different schools and lived in four countries—Singapore, Hong Kong, the United States, and Thailand—by the time I was sixteen. We would move every two years or so. I started off at each school feeling painfully shy, disconnected, and alone. By the second year I would have made friends and found my groove, and then

we would move again and the cycle would start over. Because of the many times I moved away from friends, I have a hard time connecting with people intimately and I'm afraid of being abandoned.

Every time I tell my story, I feel depressed. Wouldn't you?

My aha moment came when I realized I didn't want to feel that way any longer. So I decided to see what would happen if I changed my story. I sat down and thought about my childhood, and I chose to rewrite my story, seeing everything that happened as a gift. The result was a revelation—I had an amazing childhood! Here is my new story:

I was blessed as a child with an adventurous family. We moved every two years and traveled around the world every summer. I spent most of my childhood going to great international schools in Southeast Asia, and by the time I was sixteen my family had visited or lived in twenty different countries, including Thailand, Singapore, India, Egypt, Italy, and Spain. Because of the many times we moved and traveled, I learned to be incredibly flexible and to deeply love the diversity and creativity of humans. My childhood experiences helped me relate to many different perspectives, to make friends easily, and to celebrate change.

Each time I tell this new story, I feel a sense of adventure and lots of gratitude.

The shift inside me was profound. I felt excited, opened, and powerful. Now the question is this: Which story is true—the story of my difficult childhood, or the story of my amazing childhood? The answer is surprising: both stories are true, and neither story is true.

Our stories are true because they are one description of what happened in the past, and when we invest our energy in them, we make them true for us. And they are false because they are just stories. They are not real, they are not happening now; they appear like scenes from a silent movie that are waiting for us to assign the narrative. As descriptions of the past, they are fiction, which means we can choose to change the ending, and the beginning, and the middle, all by adjusting how we see the story.

What I have also discovered is that in order to rewrite your story, you don't have to figure out how you got the beliefs or old programming that created it, because ultimately it just doesn't matter. The moment you realize you are simply following a story that you created or adopted from others long ago is the same moment in which you have the power to change it. Consciously rewriting your story is an incredible way to shift your world. But for most of us, a story can't be rewritten until it has ripened.

The Ripe Story

When we come to the place where we can see that a story is simply that, a story, and it no longer holds power over us, then we can say this is a "ripe" story. Like a ripe piece of fruit, it will fall off the vine easily when you touch it, ready to be devoured or discarded. A story is ripe when we are no longer attached to it, when it no longer defines who we are. Stories ripen when we no longer need to believe them.

Here is a short example of a story that a friend of mine told herself for years. It illustrates how a story that initially caused suffering later ripened and could be rewritten. My friend, whom I'll call Beth, grew up thinking she was the "not smart" child in her family. She felt she was constantly being compared to her brother and his academic successes, and when she didn't do as well in school as he did, she felt unworthy and unloved by her family. The situation came to a head in college, where he excelled and she chose to drop out. After that, she entered the workforce, had a few retail jobs, and then was hired as a receptionist for a small tech company. That's where her career began to take off. Over the next fifteen years, she assumed many different positions in the company and became incredibly successful, eventually becoming an executive for the company and making a six-figure income.

It was about this time that she was also doing some serious inner work, and in the process she realized that she had made an unconscious agreement with herself many years earlier. Beth believed that if she could just achieve a certain level of professional and financial success, that this would finally prove to her family that she was smart and worthy of their love (and by default, her own).

By discovering this deep-seated belief, she was able to step out of the story that she needed to compete with her brother for the approval of her family and herself. The story had ripened within her, and she could see the truth that she was always smart, she was always worthy and lovable, and she didn't need to achieve any outward success to prove this to herself or anyone else.

With a ripened story, Beth could evaluate her current work life and decide if the long hours she was putting in were really for her, or if she was instead still trying to prove something. The story no longer had power over her, so she looked on it and herself with compassionate eyes. Because the story was ripe, Beth could choose to rewrite or discard the story.

As a side note, it's not really important whether Beth was "right" about her family comparing her to her brother. The point here is that she *believed* this to be the case and created a whole narrative around that. The story became ripe when Beth was able to see the narrative and no longer feel like it had power over her actions in the present.

Loving the Unripe Stories

In contrast, an unripe story is one that we still have a lot of emotion and energy invested in. We may want to release it, but it's not yet time. The story is still hard and bitter-tasting if we open it up. Stories like these still hurt us, because we can't see through them clearly. When we believe a story, we invest our emotional energy into it, and that keeps it growing, alive, and strong. And that's okay—because the Warrior Goddess Way is about loving all parts of yourself, and this includes the stories that are unripe.

I've learned that unripe stories hurt most when we judge ourselves for having them and try to pull them off the vine before they are ready. I've watched women create a lot of suffering over their unripe stories, and I've created a lot of suffering for myself trying to fight unripe stories.

Here are some common unripe stories that we as women tend to punish ourselves for not releasing:

- I should just be able to let my sexual abuse/rape/ domestic violence story go.

- I shouldn't still be upset about my abortion/miscarriage/inability to have children.

- It's been X months/years—I should listen to my friends and just get over my divorce/the death of my partner/the loss of my child.

On the Warrior Goddess path, we love unripeness as much as ripeness, because not doing so simply causes more internal suffering, and it is part of the old model of change we discussed in the previous chapter: "To change who I am, I need to punish myself for who I am now." Here, again, I speak from personal experience. Below is an example of a time when I first wanted to punish myself into changing but later remembered the importance of standing in my unripeness with gratitude and love.

In one of the big turning points of my life, my first husband moved out and I found myself cycling a story over and over again: *How could he leave me? I should have been different so he wouldn't leave. I'm terrible in relationships. I could have prevented this somehow.* Even though I saw the end of our relationship coming, I was in shock and turmoil for months. I had a very difficult time letting go of our marriage and our teaching and business partnership. I didn't want to. The story that we "should" be in a relationship was strong (we were married, which my old agreement kept screaming "should" be forever) even though it was no longer a reality.

I found myself one day at a crossroads. There was a part of me that wanted to push the story down and all the emotions that came with it. I wanted to be a strong, centered, powerful Warrior Goddess woman who could shake off the loss and get back to work. I had a fleeting thought: *Well, I should just move on from this already! I should be the spiritual, holy, untouchable person I am supposed to be. I should be different. People are expecting me to get over this and be bright and sunny again.*

Fortunately, my awareness kicked back in, and the word *should* was my cue. Suddenly, I remembered how I had spent so much of my life abandoning myself by thinking I should be different, and that my story should be different. I could feel that the real healing would come by not ignoring the story or covering it over with affirmations or spiritual words, but by choosing not to abandon myself. That day I made a pact with myself that I would take as long as I needed in the healing process.

And the amazing thing is that once I gave myself permission to be with the story fully, the grip it had on me lessened. I found myself experiencing huge compassion for myself and for all people who had lost a relationship and felt devastated, confused, and fearful. I felt the tenderness of being human, and of our beautiful hearts that loved so much. I got curious about my healing process. I listened to what I needed in each moment. I stepped out of judgmental "should" and into a loving now.

Because I chose to be with my story in the moment rather than force a change in it or deny its existence, it ultimately began to ripen and I was able to release my "marriage should be forever" story and embrace being single again. Because I made a commitment to be more loving toward myself and my story, I found myself actually feeling empowered by my self-acceptance, comfortable with my pace and process, and more tender toward everyone who was struggling with a breakup, loss, or fear.

What I have learned is that anytime we say, "I shouldn't feel this way," we are essentially saying "I shouldn't have this story." But if you look closely, you'll notice this too is a form of self-rejection, as the mind has found another way you *should* be different. This point is so important that it bears repeating: anytime you hear yourself say the words "I should," take a breath and show up with yourself. Can you practice having a compassionate acceptance of your self and your story, instead of judging yourself for having it?

When we come into witness and love our unripe stories, we are simply present with what is, and we treat our inner stories with the same presence and care we might give a broken bone or a cut. We know the healing will happen, and that it will take time, compassion, and a willingness to make adjustments to create the space for ripening.

Stories and Their Effects

There are times when the pain from an unripened story is so great that we can't even see the myriad ways in which the story and its unripeness are affecting us. For example, I met a woman at a Warrior Goddess workshop who stayed after class to talk to me. After conversing for a few minutes, she told me, "I am still struggling with my self-worth. I've tried so many things to feel good about myself, but it is still such a challenge." I sensed there was a lot more going on inside her than what she had shared with me so far, so I gave her my full presence, opened my heart even more to her, and asked, "Where do you think this deep sense of unworthiness comes from?"

Her eyes glistened with tears as she began telling me her story. "Well, it started when I was a little girl. You see, my father was in the military, and there were so many rules in our household. I was always breaking some rule or another. When my father perceived that I had broken a rule, he would bring me into a room and tell me that he wanted to kill me. Then he would go into great detail and describe how he would do it. And then he would tell me, 'But you aren't worth killing for the trouble I would get into.' Then he would let me go. I think that's where this all started. I have felt so unloved and unworthy for years," she continued. "I loved my father so much, and I just wanted his approval."

I breathed with her and took both her hands into mine. Here was a deeply, traumatically engrained story that she was trying to move past. Her next question to me was, "How do I make this go away?" And my response was honest. "This is deep trauma, and it's important to be gentle with yourself. Don't try to rush your healing. I support you in continuing to nourish and love yourself and show compassion for the girl that you were. Love her—let her feel your love rather than your desire to make this story go away. Know that she may always be with you, trying to feel worthy, trying not to make a mistake, trying not to get punished. Don't abandon her."

I looked into her eyes, now feeling tears glistening in mine. "And know that his story wasn't about you. You are magnificent. I see that. Your father had his own story that was based on his own past and traumas. That doesn't have to be your story."

My interaction with this young woman illustrates a foundational principle of the Warrior Goddess Way. Showing up for ourselves means that we release any ideas that we should be feeling something or being something other than who and where we are right now. Can you learn to love and honor all your feelings, rather than wish them away? This means you love unripeness as much as you love ripeness. Nothing is wrong; your story is simply not ripe, and having patience and compassion with yourself and any unripe stories can deepen your compassion for others. This is a powerful place to attend to your own ripening: by loving the unripe and nourishing ripeness, with no exception or expectation that it should be different.

Ways Our Stories Ripen

When I teach about the power of stories, I am often asked if there is a way we can speed up the ripening process. While there are things you can do (and I will go over them here), I want to stress the importance of loving and accepting yourself as you are right now. This means that once you have identified a story that is unripe, remember that the first thing is to love and honor where you are in the moment, and this includes accepting the unripeness of the story. When you look deeper at an unripe story, you can see that it serves a purpose: this story has helped you to create a sense of understanding about some situation in your world, even if it has also caused you to suffer. Finding the value in your stories allows you to practice loving them.

To begin examining the ways you can help ripen a story, let's go back to our fruit metaphor. If you have an unripe avocado, apple, or banana, there are several ways to help the ripening process along. The same is true with our stories; a Warrior Goddess has several tools at her disposal.

Patience

The first tool is patience. Much like fruit, stories can ripen naturally, over time, without our involvement. When we bring our undivided, openhearted patience to our unripened stories, we give ourselves the gift of letting time and our own faith guide us in the ripening, at our pace. This means not trying to force or rush the ripening process, but trusting the divine grace of timing. We simply look at the story when it arises and accept that it's there. We don't try to fight it, or rush it, or do anything with it. We just have love and compassion for it.

Light

The second tool is light. Fruit ripens in the sun, and the same is true for our stories. I used to leave partially green tomatoes from my garden on a sunny kitchen table, and I loved watching them turn bright red over a few days. We can do the same with our stories: bring them from the shadows into the sunlight. Writing about them, talking about them, letting them be seen and heard rather than stuffed in the darkness of our minds. Follow your stories to their depths, and bring any fears you find there to the light. Bringing your stories into the light is not about blame, shame, or should haves, as these are the ways stories stay in the shadows. Rather, letting them be witnessed and received without judgment allows the heat of acceptance—your own or someone else's—which permeates and melts the old structures.

Space

The third way to ripen fruit is to put it in a brown paper bag. As some fruit ripens, it produces a gas called ethylene. A brown paper bag traps the ethylene inside and accelerates ripening. For some stories, going into stillness and silence—taking a brown paper bag moment to center and collect yourself—will quicken the ripening. This might mean meditating, going for a long walk, or spending time alone. Taking time to unplug, reflect, and sort things out can be a crucial part of ripening your stories. In meditation and silence the mind slows down, and you are better able to see the story for what it is, clearly and rationally.

So often, we try to bury our unripe stories under layers of busyness. When you give yourself permission to retreat from the world and slow down, you can create space and stillness around the hard, green stories. This gives them room to breathe. Try sitting on your porch and holding compassion for yourself and your story. Or take long walks by yourself and imaging holding the part of you that is hurting. Or spend a few days in silent retreat, just being, without trying to fix or change or deny the unripe stories. Let the natural wisdom from the depths of your stillness soften and bring color to what was once bitter.

Sangha

The final way to ripen fruit is to put it next to other ripe fruit. Ripe fruit encourages ripeness all around it. So when you spend time with "ripe" people, their ripeness will help you to ripen. Look for people who have either been through a similar situation or have more experience than you in the particular area you are working with. I can't say enough about this. When you want to live a certain way, aligning yourself with others who are living that way can be extremely helpful.

As many of you know, I grew up in Southeast Asia, where the primary religion is Buddhism. One of the three foundational tenets of Buddhism is the *sangha*, which can be translated as "a group of like-minded individuals." Most spiritual traditions understand the power of community when it comes to transformation, as it's often easier to make changes when we are supported and encouraged by others on the same path. This same principle is true when it comes to ripening your story.

So, if you want more abundance in your life and your old story is about not having what it takes, spend time around people who are abundant and who believe in you. If you feel that more love is the key that will help unlock the bind of your story, spend time around loving people. You can also watch videos or read books from ripe people who are sharing their gifts. Every little bit helps our bodies to ripen.

Finally, another key to ripening a story can be found in forgiveness. As you forgive a person or situation, you remove the emotional energy you have invested in it, freeing you to become who you are meant to be. We will look at the Warrior Goddess path of forgiveness in the next chapter. But before we do, let's look at some explorations to help you identify and love your stories.

Wisdom: Story Resources
Gifts

 ◆ The stories we tell ourselves inform who we think we should be. When we learn to witness our stories, we can reclaim ourselves as dynamic storytellers and learn to shift our perspective.

 ◆ Compassion and patience help us to hold both the ripe and the unripe stories with love.

- Learn to love and honor all your feelings rather than wish them away.

Explorations

IDENTIFYING YOUR UNRIPE STORIES

For the next week, carry a little journal around with you. The first time you notice a story, write it down. Then, whenever you repeat a story, put a mark next to it in your journal. When you hear yourself say, "I shouldn't have this story" or "I should be done with this already," add a star next to it. At the end of the week, look at which stories have the most marks and stars. These are your unripe stories.

BLESSING THE STORY

Come present with a story you are telling yourself that no longer serves you. How does the story make you feel? How does it make you respond? Get to know the story, both on the inside with how you feel and on the outside with how you act. Write it down.

Once you've written the story, imagine it is a person who is afraid or confused. Talk to the story as if it were alive. Show up for the story. Be fully present: "Hi, story. How are you today? I see that you are feeling scared and you've decided nothing is going to work. I wanted to let you know I see you, and I am here with you." Write a love letter to your story. Or act out your story with passion, exaggerating the tale so it is an epic, beautiful drama. Or build an altar for your story, complete with flowers and candles.

By blessing your story in one or more of these ways, you can step back and get some distance. Look at your story from a different point of view. What do you learn? What wisdom arises for your healing?

FRUIT WISDOM

Next time you are in the grocery store, hold ripe fruit in one hand and unripe fruit in the other. Appreciate both the ripe and unripe. Show up for both equally. This may seem silly, but I promise you the physical practice of learning to accept ripe and unripe fruit will help you to be present with both your ripe and unripe stories.

THREE

The Wisdom of Forgiveness

As long as you don't forgive, who and whatever it
is will occupy a rent-free space in your mind.
—Isabelle Holland

I magine for a moment what it would be like to carry around a five-pound bag of potatoes with you everywhere you went. And by everywhere, I mean everywhere. To work, into the bathroom, to the grocery store. For the first week or two, the bag would just be heavy and awkward. But then things would get worse, because as the potatoes grew older they would go bad and begin to stink.

I don't know about you, but the idea of carrying around a five-pound bag of mushy, stinky, and decomposing potatoes sounds pretty rotten (pun intended!), and most of the women I know would never do such a thing. But the irony is that many of us do carry around a heavy burden of hurt, anger, judgment, and resentments toward others and ourselves wherever we go.

The wisdom of forgiveness, of others and yourself, is an act of self-love that allows you to put the rotting, smelly, oozing bag of past potatoes down. This is one of the most important chapters in the book, because if you learn and practice the wisdom of forgiveness, you can radically change your world in ways you can't even imagine. Let's start this lesson on forgiveness by examining it through the attributes of a Warrior Goddess.

A warrior forgives because she doesn't want to carry any baggage that will weigh her down. She recognizes that holding grudges or blaming others only hurts her. She knows that sometimes it's necessary to fight back, but she does so only as a last resort. A warrior wants to be free of the past so she can move effortlessly and travel wherever she wants, unafraid of who or what she might see on the way. She forgives herself and others for the events of the past, learning as she goes and adjusting her actions accordingly.

A goddess forgives because she wants the spaciousness inside to love. Harboring pain over someone else's unconscious actions or unskillful words creates heaviness inside her and is a barrier to practicing love. Forgiveness dissipates the inner stagnation of hurt and washes her clean to embody compassion and peace. A goddess wants to celebrate each moment, and so she forgives herself and others for the events of the past, opening her heart to the imperfections and pain of humans, softening as she goes and choosing love over revenge.

These are the forgiveness ideals of a Warrior Goddess, so let us remember them as we move through the rest of this chapter. But first, let's look at what forgiveness is *not*.

What Forgiveness Is Not

Being forgiving does not mean you become a pushover and let someone walk all over you because you have "forgiven him/her." That is not true forgiveness, nor is it the path of the Warrior Goddess. Forgiveness is an active state of being, not a passive one, and when we approach it that way we also get clarity on how we want to proceed with the other party involved.

In other words, choosing to grant forgiveness may also mean making a boundary or ending a relationship. Remember, Warrior Goddesses, you can forgive someone and say good-bye to them too.

One of the most difficult aspects of forgiveness is understanding that others have a right to make the choices they are making (even when we disagree or are even horrified by their choices), and we also know that we have the right to make our own choices too. Forgiveness, like the stories we discussed in the last chapter, also has a ripening phase. Forgiveness is ripe when we realize we've chosen to carry the putrefying potatoes and are now ready to put them down. Forgiveness is not ripe for the picking when we are still recovering from the hurt, believing the story, or clinging to being right (or being wrong).

Just like with your stories, it is important that you honor the ripeness of your forgiveness. If you are not ready to forgive and you try to force forgiveness because you think you "should" or because you think that's what it means to be a "spiritual person," then that's not really forgiving, that's forcing. That is not the Warrior Goddess Way. Remember, we accept, love, and respect ourselves when we aren't ready to forgive, and we also recognize that we can carry those potatoes around until we don't want to anymore.

To reiterate an earlier point, if you are being physically or emotionally abused, I don't want you to think that you should forgive the other person and then continue to let them abuse you. That is you choosing to abuse yourself by staying in a repetitive pattern. Give yourself permission to walk away or set boundaries. Get help if you need to. There are many domestic violence support groups and centers you can reach out to.

Forgiveness Untruths

In my work with women over the past several years, I have noticed there are a handful of common untruths that keep us from practicing forgiveness. I call these untruths because when we look deeper at them we find that all are rooted in old stories that don't serve our evolution on the Warrior Goddess path. Let's examine these untruths one by one.

If I Forgive, I Am Condoning the Behavior

Forgiving someone does not mean you agree with their choices or their actions. Forgiveness means you understand that you, along with all other humans, sometimes make poor choices and act in ways that are hurtful to others. While you are not agreeing with their behavior, bringing forgiveness to a situation breaks the endless cycle of judgment and punishment that only perpetuates unconscious actions. With forgiveness, you name the other person's humanity and bring in the possibility of healing, rather than demonizing them and perpetuating the pain.

The Other Person Needs to Apologize Before I Can Forgive Them

Waiting for someone else to apologize for their behavior is like holding on to the handle of a hot skillet and telling someone else to let go. "You're hurting me," you say, "so apologize so I can feel better." But the truth is that you are grasping an experience that is wounding you and causing pain. Again, you don't have to agree with their behavior to forgive them—and you also don't need their apology to forgive.

It is so freeing when you can face someone who has hurt you through their actions and, despite their denial, anger, or behavior, choose to release them from your psyche. Remember, they are hurting inside, which is causing their behavior. When you put the hot skillet of the past down and forgive even when they refuse to apologize, you stop the burn from searing you any further.

Forgiving someone in spite of their state of consciousness is a way of separating yourself from them. You are two individuals. They have a choice in how they behave. And you also have a choice in how you behave. Don't link your choice to theirs and keep suffering. Open your hand, release your grasp on the story, and let your love heal the wound.

I Have a Right to Be Hurt, and They Don't Deserve to Be Forgiven

When someone wrongs you, you absolutely have the right to feel resentful and hurt. What they did may have been terrible. But is that really how you want to spend your day? How does it feel to experience the stab of pain, the grief, or the resentment every time you think about this person, hear their name, or bump into them at the corner store or a social gathering?

Our inner dialogue often thrives on being right: I am right, they are wrong. I am the victim, he or she is the perpetrator. I am good, they are bad. This type of black-and-white thinking feels falsely empowering and clear because it leaves no messy gray areas. But dichotomies such as right and wrong and good and bad only exacerbate our suffering. In order to stay "right" we must stay the victim, continuously feel the negative emotions of that story, and look for all the ways we were harmed. In order for them to stay "wrong" we have to continue to see only their act of betrayal and hurt, not their unconsciousness. This is not inclusive thinking, and ultimately it doesn't allow for healing to occur in ourselves or in those around us.

What They Did Was So Egregious It's Unforgivable

Some particularly horrific actions are understandably the most difficult obstacle for women to overcome, but even here the wisdom of forgiveness can be found. This was made clear to me at a recent Warrior Goddess Weekend when an attendee whom I'll call Betsy shared her long history of sexual, emotional, and physical abuse, which culminated in her being betrayed and raped as a young woman. We all winced as Betsy shared her story, but she was calm and reflective. When one of the other women noted her demeanor, Betsy replied, "I wasn't always at peace, I assure you, but at some point I realized I wanted to be free from my past. I didn't want to carry it around anymore. And the only way to be really free was to forgive and to recognize that I had survived, and I could thrive and learn to use the difficulties of the past to be more compassionate and loving." Betsy's forgiveness allowed her to release the weight of the abuse she had experienced and bring her attention to how she wanted to live each day of her life going forward.

In dealing with all of the above untruths, it's important to remember one thing: forgiveness is for you; it's not for the other.

As women, we are often either silently carrying the emotional wounds of oppression and unconsciousness or lashing out like cornered animals when we are hurt. If left unchecked, we can become bitter, resigned, and armored as we replay old hurts in our minds and refuse to forgive the injustice. We can become heavy with the baggage of unanswered questions: *Why? Why? Why?* We end up facing the past and walking backward toward our future.

Forgiveness allows us to turn and face our future with clear eyes and open hands. When we forgive, we lay down a heavy load so we can use our strength to take care of ourselves, learn from our mistakes and others', and make new choices.

Forgiveness is an art we learn, and the best place to start is with the itty-bitty grievances, so you can gain skill in forgiving the big things.

Little Forgiveness

When we think of forgiveness, most of us immediately think of those situations where we have strong resentments or have suffered severe hurt or trauma. Examining and finding forgiveness for those situations is vital for sure, but I also want to look at some of the little ways in which we can apply the art of forgiveness. As a Warrior Goddess, we want to go all the way and clear any obstacle in our path that is holding us back from living a peaceful life now—no matter how small it seems.

We can do this by becoming aware of what I call the "little forgiveness opportunities." Notice the situations where you feel irritated, resentful, or frustrated. Listen to what you are saying to yourself:

- How dare they cross the street in front of me without looking!

- I can't believe my coworker didn't finish his part of the report on time!

- They canceled my flight—what were they thinking?!?

- Why didn't he call me? Doesn't he know I'm worried?

These can seem like such normal reactions that we don't think about them in terms of forgiveness. But the amazing thing is that when you begin to practice forgiveness in all these little ways, not only do you create a more peaceful day-to-day life, but you actually are able to handle forgiving larger issues more easily. But just like with the self-judgments in chapter 1, we can train our minds to reach for forgiveness instead of resentment and righteousness in each of these circumstances by consciously choosing to see the situation through the eyes of forgiveness. For example,

- They have a right to cross the street however they want to. I forgive them.

- My coworker got behind and didn't finish on time. I forgive him.

- The airlines made a mistake and I didn't get to go on my trip. I forgive them.

- He has a right to call or not call. I forgive him.

Practicing this little forgiveness is like learning the basic chords on a piano or guitar. It takes repetition until the action becomes second nature. But once you get good at it, the music of peace flows from your heart throughout the day, regardless of what obstacles arise on your path.

Big Forgiveness

Closely related to the practice of little forgiveness is a practice I call big forgiveness. While little forgiveness comes from forgiving all the small obstacles that arise throughout the day, big forgiveness is aimed at a willingness to forgive life.

The practice of forgiving life means that we get to grant forgiveness to all frustrating, uncontrollable, and heartbreaking expressions that arise in our field of awareness: when we turn on the news and see the destruction of war; when we drive down the road and witness an animal that has been struck; when we hear about a natural disaster that caused immense pain and loss of life—if we aren't aware, we can become overtaken with the anger, sadness, or despair at events such as these, and create a story of victims and villains all over again. When this happens, we see the world as a scary place rather than a kind one. We forget that all beings are on their own path, and we can't fully understand all the twists and turns, or why life unfolds as it does. Over and over again, in both little and big ways, we practice forgiveness by naming where we are withholding our acceptance and inviting ourselves to let go.

Practicing little and big forgiveness doesn't mean you don't take action to try to change things when change is possible or feel empathy for those who are suffering; rather, you develop a skill that allows you to accept and forgive what you cannot change and be of service to others who are suffering without being consumed by the sorrow yourself. When you become overcome with sorrow or pity, you actually lose the ability to be the most helpful.

The culmination of our forgiveness practice comes from the convergence of these two parallel paths: practicing forgiving the little things over and over again and cultivating the wisdom of forgiving life. When you practice little and big forgiveness until it becomes a habit, a transformation occurs. Suddenly, you find yourself accepting life for exactly what it is, in this moment, and then simultaneously there is no need for forgiveness.

When you release life from your expectations and desires, you let yourself grow from a frustrated, sulking, or victimized child to a mature, wise elder. Again, I'm not saying you are going to love everything that life throws your way, but you *will* navigate the waters differently. The attitude of "How dare life/God/that person do this to me!" will be replaced by responding to that curveball you didn't see coming with the wisdom of your wide-open heart. And the amazing truth is that eventually, if you train your mind to forgive in this way, there will be nothing to forgive, because you realize that nothing is personal.

This is the Warrior Goddess Way of forgiveness. It starts by being gentle with yourself for where you aren't ready to forgive. It continues with noticing where you want to cultivate more forgiveness for yourself and others and ultimately granting that forgiveness because you know doing so heals you and the world in the process, and finally transforming gently, slowly, and surely into never needing to forgive again.

Wisdom: Forgiveness Resources

Gifts

- A Warrior Goddess forgives because she doesn't want to carry baggage that weighs her down.

- Forgiveness is an art that takes patience, practice, and compassion.

- When we forgive, we stop reliving the past and turn to walk with a clear, soft heart into our future.

Explorations

FORGIVENESS TALK

This forgiveness method involves a stuffed animal and a willingness to release old emotions.

Pick a person you feel ready to forgive. If you are not ready to forgive this person, wait; do not attempt this practice until you feel at least a thimbleful of willingness. Willingness does not imply that you know how to forgive, only that you are ready to open a door to new possibilities.

Pick a stuffed animal (or a rock will do) to represent the person you aim to forgive. Sit down with the stuffed animal in a chair across from you, and tell the stuffed animal, "I want to forgive you. I am willing to learn how to forgive you." Now share anything that is keeping you from forgiving. What are you afraid will happen if you forgive this person? Why do you still want to punish this person? Express any emotions that arise—cry, scream, stomp your feet, grieve. Breathe. Let go of all that you have been carrying.

Forgiveness can take time. If necessary, carry the stuffed animal around with you, or make sure to visit it frequently and have as many heart conversations as you need to shift the energy.

FORGIVING OTHERS

Forgiveness is a muscle that we can strengthen over time. Here is a way to do lots of little repetitions to build up your core capacity to forgive.

Answer the below questions in regards to others, answering the complete list of questions for each individual that still brings a heaviness to your heart. Don't think too much about each question; just answer each one as honestly as you can from where you are right now—not where you wish you were. If emotions come up, don't repress them, but sit with the feelings and see if you can pay attention to where they live in your body and how they feel.

1. Whom are you resentful or angry toward, and why? Write down the first name and a brief statement of why you are upset. For example, you might say the following: *Tom—he cheated on me.*

2. Are you ready to try to forgive them? Remember, there is no right or wrong answer here. Go inside and see if you are ready to try to forgive them. *Try* is the important word, because it doesn't mean you will be able to do so yet. And if you're not yet ready to try, that's fine too. If you are ready to try to forgive them, write that down like this: *I am ready to forgive Tom for cheating on me.* If you are not ready to forgive, write that down: *I am not ready to forgive Tom for cheating on me.*

3a. If you *are* ready to try to forgive, answer this question: Why do you want to forgive? In other words, what are the benefits of forgiving? Take a moment to write down what forgiveness means to you and why you'd like to cultivate it in your life.

3b. If you *are not* ready to try to forgive, answer this question: Why do you not want to forgive? In other words, what are the benefits of not forgiving? Write down why you're holding on to the feelings that you have. What are they doing for you? This doesn't mean you are wrong to hold them; the point of this question is to find out what you are getting out of it.

Now that you are clear on the people you want to extend forgiveness to, why, and if you're ready to act, pay attention to what it feels like when you think of those you don't want to forgive today versus those you do. How do these feel differently in your body? What emotions do you experience when you think about the two different groups?

Here are some examples of forgiveness from the Warrior Goddess community:

> I forgave my best friend for the night I found her in bed with a man I thought I was in love with. It hurt, and I distanced myself from her for over a year, but we are now close again. I'm so happy to have her in my life. She is for sure a soul mate—and the guy is long gone. I also forgave him. He taught me strength. I feel incredibly powerful because of the things I learned in that relationship.

> My ex-husband stole my financial identity and stole money from clients all through a business we owned. He had lied to me for at least a year, with elaborate cover-ups and distractions. When I found out, my sons were three and one and a half. My boys are now eighteen and almost seventeen. I do not trust my ex. But I have forgiven him, because I moved on to so many great things as a result of living through that experience. I wouldn't have done

it differently. I'm proud of who I am and where I am in my life, and I wouldn't have that if I had held on to the things he did.

~

Forgiving family members has helped me heal and move on in my life path. I spend less energy devoted to remembering suffering and mulling over why things happened. Now I use my newly freed up energy for positive things, including building the best relationship possible with the same family members, while trying to avoid building a relationship based on fantasy or ignoring the limitations of the person/history/situation.

Anytime you notice yourself contracting, judging, or blaming, ask yourself this question: What would forgiveness feel like here? You might not get an immediate answer or have the grace of forgiveness rain down upon you. You will be carving new channels in your being that will allow forgiveness to flow over time. Keep exploring, asking, and listening.

We'll do a forgiveness mantra for those you are ready to try to forgive in a moment. But before we do that, let's look at another person who often needs your forgiveness—yourself.

FORGIVING YOURSELF

Let's apply the same set of questions as before to areas where you are holding something against yourself.

Looking back at your life, in what areas or situations do you think you have "failed' or otherwise beat yourself up? Remember, much like the self-judgments we discussed in chapter 1, some of these self-resentments can be sneaky and subtle, so in addition to the most obvious incidents that come to mind be sure to look closely at the little stories of failure you hold against yourself and replay from time to time.

Once you have identified the places you are still holding something against yourself, I want you to get still for a moment and ask yourself, "Are you ready to try to forgive yourself in each of these instances?" Just like in the previous section, write out whether you are ready to forgive yourself or not. Here are some examples shared by the Warrior Goddess community:

I cheated on my former husband. I am ready to try to forgive myself.

I dropped out of college and often think I am a failure for doing so. I am ready to forgive myself.

I am ready to forgive myself for pursuing men in relationships who don't want me.

I am ready to forgive myself for my challenges with food.

I am ready to forgive myself for all the judgments I have made and held firmly that were absolutely untrue and destructive.

I married a man I didn't realize was alcoholic, and it impacted my young son awfully at the time. I'm ready to try to forgive myself.

I handed my power to someone else because I believed they could do it all so much better than I could and I was afraid of the responsibility. I am ready to forgive myself for that.

I am ready to forgive myself for not having a partner in life. I forgive myself for thinking that I have to do it all alone.

Repeat the questions from the previous section for each past action that you have been using to deny yourself acceptance and love. What does it feel like when you think of those areas where you don't want to forgive yourself? What does it feel like when you think of those areas where you *are* ready to forgive yourself? How do these feel differently in your body? What emotions do you experience when you think about the two different groups?

FORGIVENESS MANTRA

If there are places where you aren't yet ready to forgive either yourself or others, that's okay. As a Warrior Goddess you love ripeness and unripeness. For those people and instances where you are ready to try to forgive, now is the time and this is the place to begin to do so.

Write a statement of forgiveness and address it to the person you would like to forgive. Say what you want to forgive them for. Below are some examples of how to do this:

I forgive _____ for _____. I no longer
want to hold any heaviness in my heart of this. I
release all of my resentments over this and wish
_____ peace.

Read the above statement out loud. For some of you,
doing so may feel insincere at first. This is where the try part
comes in.

Next, write out that same statement in relation to yourself.

I forgive myself for _____. I no longer want
to hold any heaviness in my heart of this. I release all
of my resentments over this and wish myself peace.

If you are like me, you may find that forgiving yourself
often occurs simultaneously when you begin to forgive others. That's because when you hold something against someone
else, you also hold that same behavior against yourself; and
when you release that behavior against someone else, you also
become willing to forgive yourself.

For example, let's say you are upset with someone because
they lied to you. I bet you can find a time in your past when
you also told a lie. It doesn't matter if their lie was "worse";
the point is that as long as you hold the resentment, you'll find
that you hold the same action against yourself in some other
circumstance.

So what would forgiveness look like in this situation?
Perhaps you can see that the other person acted out of fear,
pain, imperfection, and unconsciousness, and you accept
that this was who they were in the moment. Remember, this
doesn't mean you automatically believe what they say in future

dealings with them, as your boundary may be to not believe them. Forgiveness occurs when you realize that they lied, and it is pointless for you to still hurt as a result. You understand that the lie is what it is, and you see that you have lied in the past too. The most important component is this: you no longer wish them ill over the past event. You can see them and are no longer bothered by it. That's forgiveness in action. As you get stronger at this, you may even begin to wish them well.

FOUR

The Wisdom of Apology

Right actions in the future are the best
apologies for bad actions in the past.
—Tryon Edwards

N ow that we have looked at the wisdom of forgiveness
and how practicing it benefits you, others, and the
world, it's time to explore the wisdom of apology, because this
is an area in which women in particular often need a make-
over. I was one of those women. I used to be the one who
would apologize if someone stomped on my foot and felt
responsible, and I often apologized if someone near me was
having a bad day. This habit of apologizing for everything is
so pervasive with women, and I find that the habit of unconsciously apologizing still sneaks up on me from time to time.
For instance, the other day I almost started a blog by apologizing for not writing sooner.

Can you relate?

Many women I know can, as apologizing for our very existence seems to be hardwired into us at a pretty early age. That's
not too difficult to understand when you consider that the pre-
dominant religious creation story of our culture squarely puts
the blame on a woman for being the cause of casting future

generations out of paradise. Whoops. It's as if we have been apologizing and asking for forgiveness ever since!

And even the women I know who don't have a habit of verbally apologizing for every little thing still often find that they too take on guilt or blame for things that they aren't responsible for, such as the anxiety, sadness, or sometimes even actions of others. So whether you are someone who says you're sorry out loud or you just feel responsible on the inside, the beginning of this chapter is devoted to identifying and releasing the ways in which you apologize. This is your next stop on the path of Warrior Goddess wisdom.

The key to changing this pattern, and all patterns, can be found in the words *notice* and *witness*. When you notice or witness something, this means you do so without judgment, and without trying to change it (yet). You are like a scientist studying yourself, and this detached observing allows you to see what, when, and why you do something. Awareness is the first step to change.

Remember, you weren't born apologizing or feeling responsible for others; these are things you've learned over time. Changing our unconscious agreements and actions can go from awareness to transformation when we stop judging ourselves and simply perceive what is, in this moment, with curiosity. As you notice all the little places you either apologize or feel responsible for outcomes or others' happiness through-out your week, ask yourself, "What am I really apologizing for?" and "Why do I feel responsible for this?" Go deeper and explore the foundational agreements you are carrying.

For example, as I watched myself and got curious about why I apologized, I discovered an old agreement: "It's not okay to make people uncomfortable with what I say or do—I need to please people." I watched how at times I would unconsciously try to make myself smaller and pull my energy back so I wouldn't upset or affect others, all in an attempt to make them happy, even if that meant doing so at my own expense. Another old agreement I unearthed was, "It's my job to try to fix others," which left me feeling sorry and apologetic when I couldn't. Since no one can really fix anyone else, I ended up feeling this way a lot. Do either of these deep-seated agreements sound familiar to you?

In general, you might not find your deeper agreements right away, and that is fine. Keep being curious, holding the question in your being, watching your behaviors and reactions, and noticing what you do with your body and your energy when you apologize. If you unearth an old subterranean agreement, bring it into the light of day. Allow it to ripen, or use the unripeness as medicine. Even the hard, bitter fruit has value.

Your compassion, your love, your presence is the heat that ignites the ripening process or the warmth of understanding and patience that holds your unripeness tenderly. Both are to be respected and honored as teachers and even friends.

If you are someone who habitually or unconsciously apologizes, simply begin to notice where you do so. Be curious. Where and when do you say you are sorry without even realizing it? Don't try to change anything, just witness yourself in relation to others. And for those of you who don't verbally say you are sorry, notice where you try to fix a problem that you didn't cause and take on some sense of responsibility to do so. This doesn't mean you don't try to be helpful when you can, but notice when you are trying to manage a situation, attempting fix a problem, or making someone feel a certain way when it may not be your place or within your power to do so.

Saying Sorry for Real

There are times when an apology, either an attempt to make something right or an acknowledgment of sorrow, can truly be helpful. Once we become aware of and stop the energy leak of apologizing or feeling responsible for everything, from breathing to taking up space, we can then see when apologizing would actually be appropriate, and also learn how to apologize sincerely.

In my view, there are three instances when saying the words "I'm sorry" is appropriate, and learning when and how to do so is a key to taking responsibility for yourself and owning your actions. Being a Warrior Goddess means taking responsibility, and sometimes that means rendering an apology for your actions or sharing an expression of sorrow. And remember, there is a difference between beating yourself up and noticing where you have done or said something you now need to correct. The former comes from self-rejection, while the latter comes from self-love. Because you love and honor yourself, you can actually love and honor others, and this means taking responsibility for things that you *are* responsible for.

Let's discuss a few of the ways we can sincerely apologize. There are three instances when an apology or expression of sorrow is appropriate. We apologize when

1. We've done something that's negatively impacted others.

2. We want to express our sympathy.

3. We want to make a deep heart apology for a
   past action.

It's important to keep your awareness open so you can determine when you're consciously apologizing versus when you're unconsciously saying something to appease someone else, diminishing yourself in the process.

We've Done Something That's Negatively Impacted Others

The first instance of sharing a sincere "sorry" mends the tear when you make a mistake that affects someone. Let's say you bump into someone and spill your drink on them. These are situations that arise in the moment because you, like everyone else, make mistakes (remember this statement from chapter 1?). This type of apology acknowledges your humanness, and you are attempting to make it right. If what you did affected someone else, you don't need to punish yourself endlessly or grovel before them. Just take a breath, look them in the eye, connect with your heart, and say, "I am sorry." Keep eye contact. Breathe. Stay with yourself.

In these instances, it's important to remember that you are not responsible for the other party's *reaction* to your mistake. For instance, if you spill your drink on someone by accident and immediately say you are sorry, and they say, "What is the matter with you?! My night is ruined!" you can see that their reaction is their story. It has gone beyond the scope of your involvement. It is not your job to pick up the bait and feel responsible for the rest of it.

The drink example is an easy one, but when we turn to situations that involve those closest to us, our tendency may still be to take on more than our fair share. For instance, I have a friend who unexpectedly had to work late because a coworker got sick, and this resulted in her being unable to drive her teenage daughter to a social outing. She apologized to her daughter for being unable to take her, to which her daughter responded, "I can't believe you're doing this to me! I never get to do anything! You're a horrible mother!" My friend called my very upset. She felt responsible for her daughter's heartache, but together we looked at what she was and was not responsible for. Her duty in this situation was to put food on the table, and that meant honoring her job over her commitment to her daughter's social calendar (or her overly dramatic response).

We Want to Express Our Sympathy

Saying a heartfelt "I'm sorry" can also act as a soothing balm when someone shares that they are dealing with a difficult situation. This is really an acknowledgment of the difficulty and suffering that another one is facing, and you are being present for them and expressing your compassion toward them. An "I see you, I feel you, I honor with gratitude the richness of being human" apology creates connection and intimacy and expands our heart.

I recently had an intimate conversation with a friend who revealed to me the tenderness of his grief around the death of his brother. I felt his grief, felt my compassion and past grief, took a breath, looked him in the eye, and said, "I am sorry." I didn't try to fix his pain, diminish it, or talk about my pain. People want our presence, not our caretaking or rapid-fire stories. A deep, present "I am sorry" gives others the gift of being seen and received where they are.

It's important as Warrior Goddesses that we notice the energetic difference between apologizing as an expression of personal responsibility and apologizing as an acknowledgment of sorrow. In the latter, we aren't responsible for the situation, so our energy is one of conscious compassion, sharing in the plight of another human.

When we step toward our humanity, we willingly turn toward the experiences of grief, pain, and loss that touch us all. As long as we are in a human body, there is no getting away from the sacred inevitability of death, aging, and illness, no avoiding the unexpected tragedy. But instead of letting these life experiences cause us fear or dread, we can let them hollow us out so we can hold more love, gratitude, and reverence for all of the cycles.

Let yourself feel the pain and grief of others while breathing through your heart and staying open. Don't minimize or dramatize their experience. Let them be exactly where they are. Nothing is wrong; nothing needs to be fixed. Then you can practice opening even wider to honor all the beings who are in pain or struggling with similar issues.

We Want to Make a Deep Heart Apology for a Past Action

There are also cases, especially those that may have come up in the forgiveness exercise earlier, where we look back at our past actions or words and know in our heart we did something that we now know was unconscious. We may have forgiven ourselves for it already, but as a Warrior Goddess we want to do our part to not only heal ourselves but also any hurt we have caused in the world. In this way, what I call a gut level, deep heart "I'm sorry" can clear old baggage from the past. The key here is that your intent is to take responsibility for past actions with the hope to rectify any damage done, as much as that is possible.

Again, the key here is that we are ready to own our part in any action we have done. But we also want to be careful we don't assume responsibility for the other person's reactions. One way to navigate this is when you are ready to apologize, be sure to stick to the facts, as doing so can release you from interpreting the event for the other person. Remember, you ultimately can't know their perspective. For instance, state clearly, "I lied to you about XYZ, and I am sorry for that," or "I said or did XYZ, and that was inappropriate of me. I apologize." These are the facts, not stories about what the facts mean, which can keep you focused.

Another important point when making an apology is to talk about your actions only, not anyone else's. You also don't want to offer excuses for your behavior. For instance, if you say, "I'm sorry for doing ABC, but if you hadn't done XYZ, I wouldn't have reacted that way," this is an example of what's called a "conditional" apology, and it's not really from your heart. If you are only willing to make an apology with a condition, then this simply means the apology isn't ripe in you yet. That's fine, but I suggest putting off that apology until the story around it has ripened.

Conscious apologizing can open up amazing new doors in your life. When I was around twenty-four, I talked badly about someone in our community that I was really upset by. At the time I didn't think much of it, but I learned of the ramifications when twenty years later I reached out via email and apologized to him for spreading poison in the past. He responded to my email with a long letter sharing how because of things I said he was ostracized and vilified by many people around him. At the time I felt powerless and didn't realize the impact of my anger at him and how it would affect our community and his life. I called him and thanked him for sharing the impact my unconscious victimization and toxic words had created, and I apologized again from my heart. I recently ran into him, and we had the most tender heart connection and conversation. We didn't bring up the past, and I could feel that both of us were so grateful for the healing of an apology given sincerely and received fully.

Lastly, there are those cases where a direct apology is not helpful or simply not an option. For instance, if offering an apology would cause more pain and suffering to the one you are seeking to make things right with, then it's best to leave it alone. Or if approaching someone would cause you more pain and suffering, then it may be best to leave it alone. I have a friend who ended a relationship with an abusive ex, and while she felt she owed him an apology for certain things she had done, we both agreed it wasn't good for her to have any further contact with him. If an apology is not an option because the other person has passed away, or you have no way of contacting them, you may find some closure with an apology offering ritual. (See the Explorations section at the end of this chapter for how to do this.)

Depending on the situation, offering deep apologies like these can be some of the most difficult conversations we have. But when it's necessary to offer one, we put on our big girl pants and do it. The point in all three of these instances of appropriate apologies is that as Warrior Goddesses we are aware of our actions and we are aware of the suffering of others, and we use our words wisely to express our sorrow or take responsibility for our actions. By forgiving others and ourselves first, we enter a place energetically where we can offer an apology or an expression of sympathy as a conscious choice rather than a habit or reaction.

Wisdom: Apology Resources

Gifts

- Habitually apologizing drains our energy and keeps us small.

- Women often unconsciously apologize for our very existence.

- Learning to consciously apologize to others is a form of self-love and personal responsibility.

Explorations

THE NOT SORRY/I'M SO SORRY GAME

For one week or so, explore where you say "sorry" unconsciously. Don't try to change your behavior, just witness where you say "I'm sorry" on the inside or out loud. Ask yourself, "What am I really apologizing for?"

Then begin to practice not apologizing. It will probably be uncomfortable, so don't get discouraged if you feel bad or unkind. Stick with your exploration of what it feels like to stop apologizing for being alive. It will get easier, and soon you will feel more in your power.

Here are some examples from the Warrior Goddess community. Which ones do you relate to?

- The other day I apologized when my friend got a flat tire on my road.

- I apologize for the way I look all the time.

- I apologize about the state of my house when friends come over, even when it is spotless.

- When I was a kid, I mentally apologized for my father's behavior all the time, and now I apologize for my husband's actions as if they are my fault!

The second part of the game is to look for the places where a good, heartfelt apology would be of benefit. Apologize to yourself in the mirror for the ways you've betrayed, abandoned, or hurt yourself. Apologize fully, eye to eye, heart to heart, when you make a mistake that affects someone else. Say an authentic "I'm sorry" when someone is hurting. Then breathe and be with them (or with yourself). Nothing else is needed.

APOLOGY OFFERING RITUAL

Ritual offers us a deeper layer of healing, as it uses symbols and physical action to help us release and clear the old energies from our unconscious and then guides us to consciously choose where we want to put our focus.

This apology ritual can be done alone or with a partner (a friend, a beloved, a parent or child), or within a group (your women's circle, a group of friends, your family). Feel free to modify this ritual to fit your needs.

Gather the following items:

- A candle

- Matches

- A small square of paper

- A pen

- A bowl of water

- A fireproof bowl

1. Light the candle and sit quietly for a few moments, letting the rest of your day go and getting completely present.

2. When you feel ready, write down what you are apologizing for. Hold it between your hands and feel your sincere desire to apologize.

3. Place the paper under the bowl of water.

4. Use water to wash your hands, imagining that you are washing away the circumstances that caused your action or any emotions: guilt, fear, unconsciousness, shame, blame.

5. Say out loud, "With this water I release guilt from my being, and I give myself permission to let it go."

6. Now hold the paper with your apology and say out loud, "I apologize for my behavior and ask that with love I may learn from the past and be more conscious and present in the future."

7. Turn the paper over, and on the back write down what you learned and what different choices you would make now.

8. Now burn paper while you say, "I transform this apology into clarity and healing," and place it in the fireproof bowl.

9. Once the flame has gone out, take a bit of ash on your finger and put it on your heart. Imagine that you can breathe in the lesson and the transformation.

If you have a partner: Follow the steps above, but when you share your apology and what you learned, speak directly to your partner, making eye contact and seeing what wants to be shared between you.

If you are working with a group: Follow the steps above, but have each woman share her apology and what she learned in the middle of the circle, so that the circle can witness her apology and her lessons learned. If you'd like, have one person stand in to "receive" the apology and say, "I accept your apology."

Part Two

AUTHENTICITY

Authenticity is not something to strive for on the outside; it is something to embrace from the inside. You don't become authentic by being right or spiritual or good. You become authentic by embracing your vulnerability and your silliness, and owning all your superpowers. You become authentic when you accept and love where you are in the moment, especially in those times when whatever you are experiencing doesn't match the image of what you think "should be." The Warrior Goddess Way shows you how to walk the path of embodied you-ness.

The artist Michelangelo said that to create his sculptures he simply carved away all the parts that were not the essential creation within the stone. As artists of our own lives, revealing our authentic selves can be described as rolling up our sleeves, grabbing our tools, and chipping away at everything that is not essentially us. Sometimes the work is difficult, exhausting, and dirty, and other times it can seem futile, like nothing is changing or there are no visible results. But when we catch a glint of the gold of our essence within the hard rock of our own self-judgment and fears, we know that we are on the right track.

I'm going to walk along side you step-by-step, on the Warrior Goddess Way to accessing your authentic self. I will metaphorically hold your hand and share what has worked for my students and myself. But to see the results I know you want, you are going to have to be willing to go deep, get messy, and diligently and patiently chip away at all that is not you.

That likely sounds like a tall order, so here is the twist: the first step is to relax. Yes, uncovering your authentic self is probably going to include some hard, uncomfortable, and vulnerable work, but take a moment and notice your first thought: Is it to clamp down or punish and judge your way to your inner freedom? Does your body feel relaxed, excited, and eager, or tight and serious? Remember, the Warrior Goddess Way is about supporting yourself with love and patience through this inner work, not by punishing or admonishing yourself to achieve results.

Like Michelangelo, imagine you are a sculptor, and your life is like a block of stone. As you raise your hammer to start chipping away, also notice any part of you that feels afraid: *What if I can't do it? What if I make a mistake?* Smile at this part of yourself and say, "Sweetheart, I know you are afraid, but we can do this." Imagine giving this scared part of yourself a big hug, and imagine you can hear me and your supportive sisters saying, "You can do this!" Close your eyes and imagine what this support, confidence, patience, and commitment feel like in your body. Don't shove away any parts of you that feel insecure or scared. Embrace those parts of yourself as well. Call up your self-respect by facing these old fears and committing to go forward anyway.

Feel your deep patience and willingness to stay with those parts for as long as it takes to free the authentic being you are.

Finally, let's add some glitter to your tool belt and celebrate your unveiling of self. This is your life. Why not make freeing yourself a party? Let's get excited about it too!

FIVE

Authentic Respect

Expect trouble as an inevitable part of life, and when it
comes, hold your head high. Look it squarely in the eye,
and say, "I will be bigger than you. You cannot defeat me."
—Ann Landers

As women, many of us share a personal history of not being authentic about who we really are and what we really want. I've heard so many women say, "I've tried so hard to be what I thought I should be that I don't even know who I am."

Authenticity is not something that you put on like a new, sparkly dress that makes you feel and appear a certain way. "Look, now I'm wearing authenticity! How do I look?" No! Authenticity is looking at yourself in the mirror and seeing your beauty, your grief, your courage, your quirks, and your fears all with the utmost respect for the preciousness of the human that you are. Authenticity can also be described as the willingness to discover who you are at the core of your being, embracing all that you find, and bringing both your soulful essence and your quirky human self fully into the world without shame or hiding. Being an authentic, aware woman is not easy; I see it as the journey of the heroine. There are many inner beasts to befriend and lots of fear-inducing obstacles to overcome. Letting our authentic selves shine forth into the world means being willing to face our terrors of abandonment, not being liked, and doing it wrong.

If you are like many women I know, you can point to many times in your past when you did not stand up for yourself, when you didn't honor your needs, and when you did not speak your truth. Much of this is the result of our upbringing, as in the Western world women are often taught to play small, to get out of the way, to give in, and to let the desires of others take precedence. When we see these old, deeply ingrained patterns so many women hold—self-denial, letting others make choices for us, or trying to fit in at all costs—we can understand why so many of us then end up in situations where we don't respect ourselves.

The first lesson of authenticity is all about cultivating respect and using it as a tool to transform any fears that are keeping you from being the woman you want to be, which is synonymous with who you are destined to be.

The Warrior Goddess definition of the word *respect* is both broader and deeper than how the word is popularly used and understood in society today. From a Warrior Goddess standpoint, we can say we have respect for ourselves, for someone else, or for a situation when we can see ourselves, the other person, or the situation clearly. Fear is the primary obstacle to clarity, so we lose our respect anytime our fears dominate our perceptions or control our actions. This doesn't mean that when we have respect we won't sometimes be afraid, but there is a vast difference between feeling afraid and letting fear dictate our actions.

The amazing thing is that when you cultivate Warrior Goddess respect, you no longer see your fear as an obstacle, and believe it or not, you may eventually even look forward to finding places that you are afraid so you can dance through these fears rather than run from them. When I make this proclamation at workshops and lectures, I am often asked, "How do you propose that we dance through our fears? Aren't you being frivolous by not taking things seriously?"

I am not being frivolous here, and believe me, I used to take things seriously—very seriously, in fact. But my serious attitude did not have the intended results. I thought that by being serious I could work hard and figure out how to do everything "right," thereby avoiding any unpleasant experiences or outcomes in the process. But the truth is, being serious is often an unpleasant experience in itself, because we clamp down rather than open up and explore. Our focus becomes fixated on what is wrong and in avoiding our fears, rather than on celebrating what is right and moving through what scares us. This is a radial shift in our thinking and being, and the impact on how you live your life when you embody this is equally radical.

I am not suggesting that you stuff your feelings or otherwise pretend you aren't afraid in an effort to look good. That is not the Warrior Goddess Way; that is the Barbie doll way. And while Barbie may be popular for her permanent smile and those perky breasts, she is also rigid on the outside and empty on the inside. When we deny what is happening inside us, including our fears, we become like hollow plastic, a mask without any substance.

The Warrior Goddess Way is about becoming fully engaged with both the gifts and the struggles of life, and realizing that both are here to evolve us. So let's dance with all of it, because no matter what it is, it is all dancing with us.

Cultivating authentic respect is a tool that can help us walk through our fears rather than being consumed by them.

There are three areas where we can cultivate respect over fear: when dealing with life situations, when dealing with others, and when dealing with ourselves.

Respect Over Fear When Dealing with Life

I tend to learn best through direct experience. This is often instructive, but sometimes not so pleasant. Take my relationship with poison oak, which has been a master teacher for me in terms of seeing situations with respect and clarity.

The first time I learned about the potency of poison oak, I lived in the woods of Northern California, completely surrounded by the notorious three-leaved plant. I didn't particularly notice it until I literally sat on it while peeing in the bushes. For the next ten days, the poison part of the oak had my very undivided attention.

After I recovered, I spent the next month in fear of touching poison oak. That fear was helpfully fanned by friends and strangers who generously shared their own personal poison oak horror stories. I became obsessed with avoiding it: now the beautiful, soothing land I lived on suddenly was filled with green hostiles waiting to spring at me with their destructive weapons of itch. I even avoided touching my dogs, who might be harboring the enemy on their fur. Whether I was hiking or going to the outhouse, I was on high alert.

One morning as I tiptoed to the outhouse, eyes wide and head swiveling like a hypervigilant deer, I had a sudden glimpse of what I was doing and cracked up laughing. I was terrified of a little green plant! "Okay," I said out loud, "this has got to stop!" I spent the next two days simply observing my thoughts and reactions to poison oak. I was believing the stories that once you tangled with poison oak, you grew more and more sensitive to its toxins. I was replaying the worst poison oak tales over and over in my head. I was imagining a world filled with bodily suffering.

I was a fearful wreck, and I knew I had a choice to make: I could either flee to the concrete safety of a city or turn to face my leafy demons.

So I walked off the path and went to face my foe. In the crisp autumn air, the poison oak leaves were highlighted by a bright red burnish, and the trees sprinkled me with orange-yellow leaves. I found a good, healthy poison oak bush and sat down in front of it. Then I scooted closer.

I focused my gaze and questioned the poison oak plant, "How can I release this fear I have about you?"

As I opened myself up to new information and insights, I remembered a story about Native Americans eating a tiny portion of young poison oak leaves to build their immunity to the plant's toxin. I wasn't willing to risk eating poison oak, but I did want to build immunity to my fear. What did I need to digest?

As I stared at the triple-forked, oak-shaped leaves, I understood the antidote: respect.

Here was a plant that had the ability to make humans tremble at the mere mention of its name. That was powerful! Here was a foe worthy of my honor and attention.

I bowed to the poison oak bush, brushed myself off as I got up, and continued my walk to the outhouse. But now, instead of being filled with fear, I felt internally bright with the power of respect and awareness. Soon afterward, I learned that natural cures for the itchy toxins in our poison plant relatives always grow nearby. Mugwort leaves, the tannins in oak leaves, and the green goodness of plantains all soothe and help to neutralize urushiol, the phytochemical in poison oak that causes itching. And these healing plants all flourish in the same habitat as their poisonous family member. There was a deep lesson for me here: when I view a situation with respect rather than fear, I can see the options that exist right alongside the obstacles.

From that day forward I never had another bad case of poison oak again, and I now move through the woods with warrior confidence and presence. Looking at the situation through the eyes of respect, I realized it was actually the *story* that I was telling myself about poison oak that had me living in fear rather than the plant itself. Until I turned to face it and shift the narrative my mind was spinning, I was miserable. This is yet another example of how our stories, both the present short stories and the long novels of our past, will dictate our experience if we let them. Until we know better, we believe that our stories are fixed, unalterable, true representations of reality. Until we realize that we create our stories, they trap us. We cultivate respect to step into the present moment and see clearly any fearful stories we are telling ourselves about the world.

As a dear friend likes to say, "99 percent of my worst days never happened, except in my own mind." This wise observance speaks to the power of fear, because it will consume us if we let it. What we have forgotten in those fearful moments is our own innate power, and choosing to respect a situation rather than fear it actually allows us to recognize that we too have choices in any set of circumstances. When we see things clearly, we can tap into the power of our own internal resources, our own creativity, and our own wisdom. So the next time you are in a fearful situation and are being consumed by a fearful story, ask yourself what you need to respect in the situation instead, as doing so shifts you from a state of powerlessness to a place of authentic options.

Respect Over Fear When Dealing with Others

Choosing to cultivate respect over fear when dealing with others can be some of the most difficult work we do. Many of society's messages seem to equate "earning respect" with either fighting or at the very least the unflinching willingness to fight. But always choosing to fight isn't the Warrior Goddess Way of respect, as the following story illustrates.

There was once a powerful aikido master who was approached by two men while he walked alone on a darkened street. Sensing their intentions were hostile, he turned and fled. When he shared this story with his students, they were incredulous: "Why didn't you fight them? You could have easily beaten them!" The aikido master smiled good-naturedly and replied, "Students, the point of all our training is not to always fight, but rather to find the most efficient way through any difficult encounter. And in this case, running away was the best choice."

The lesson here is that exercising Warrior Goddess respect when dealing with others does not mean being in fight mode all the time. Warrior Goddess respect is about learning to see clearly into any situation and taking the best action that feels authentic to you. This is the type of respect that allows you to acknowledge and work with fear, rather than letting it work and control you.

Of course, there are situations when we must be willing to stand up and fight for our needs, in whatever appropriate forms that takes. For example, I once coached a woman who was feeling pushed around mentally and emotionally by a soon to be ex–business partner. She felt powerless and diminished, and their increasingly heated exchanges had progressed to the point where she was afraid to engage with him at all, as each interaction left her feeling more depleted and helpless.

As we sat in her living room, which was crowded with pictures and statues of the horses she loved, she cowered in her chair when she spoke of him. As we talked further, I learned she was also an accomplished horse trainer whose specialty was rehabilitating abused horses. I encouraged her to share her passion with me, and then I watched her move from a place of fear to her natural power and strength when she spoke about her long history of working with these magnificent animals. Sensing a teaching opportunity, I asked her about her specialty.

"When you are working with an abused horse, it turns and threatens to attack you. What do you do then?" I asked her.

"I remain calm, I stay centered, and I stand my ground. I know the horse is scared and only lashing out at me due to its fear. It was abused in the past, and that's why it's acting the way it is."

"What would happen if you pulled away or cowered in fear?"

"The horse would sense that and get more aggressive and violent."

"But if you stand your ground and stay in your power, the horse will learn to respect you."

"Yes," she replied, as her eyes lit up. "And that's exactly what I need to do with my ex–business partner."

I am a firm believer that we all have our own answers— sometimes we just need a friend or guide to help us find them.

When we began the conversation, my friend was frozen in the fearful belief that she was a helpless victim and that she had no options in dealing with the situation. Through our discussion, she was able to see that she already knew what to do.

In this case, seeing her former business partner through the eyes of respect meant seeing a man who was scared and lashing out in an attempt to get his way. He was reacting in the only way he knew how, which was to try to bully her and force her to do as he requested. When she realized this, she felt empowered and was ready to stand her ground.

Respecting other people does not mean that you necessarily agree with them. Respect means that you see the other person clearly for who they really are and you respond accordingly, remembering that you too have power and options. I also want to point out that in this particular case, my friend knew this man well and felt no physical threat from him (if she did, the right response would have been to call the proper authorities, as that is respect too).

When dealing with a difficult person, making the shift from fear to respect will lift you out of your familiar rut and walk you into new perceptions and actions. Respecting the other allows you to respect yourself and your abilities, enabling you to tap into the infinite source of wisdom and creative resourcefulness that lies waiting within.

Respect Over Fear When Dealing with Ourselves

Choosing respect over fear in regards to yourself can actually be more difficult than doing so with others and situations, and that's not hard to understand when you keep in mind that many of us have a history of speaking to ourselves in ways we would never allow someone else to. As we dive into cultivating Warrior Goddess authentic self-respect, our first stop is to look at two blocks to this way of being: self-deprecation and self-importance.

Self-deprecation Versus Self-importance

Spotting and releasing self-deprecation in all its manifestations is something we have already looked at throughout the Warrior Goddess path. In terms of respect, we can say we self-deprecate the moment we think we are somehow "less than" or otherwise not as valuable or as important as others. When we believe this, we denigrate our own opinions, views, and beliefs. We consider what everyone else wants without giving much thought to how it might affect us or what our needs or wants are. This is a common issue for women, but you know by now that being a Warrior Goddess means you understand that what you want, how you feel, and who you are matter. This means you can say no, you can speak your truth, and you can make decisions and take actions based on your needs rather than putting others' needs above yours.

Self-importance is the opposite, but equally flawed, viewpoint. When we are basking in self-importance, we see ourselves as better than others or that our presence, actions, opinions, views, and beliefs are more important than the person who's standing in front of us (either physically or in our mind). The trap of self-importance is one that women can sometimes have trouble seeing, so think for a moment of any little ways that you may do this. I'll share an example from my own life in a moment. The key point here is that true self-respect does not come from disrespecting others.

Self-importance and self-deprecation are actually two sides of the same counterfeit coin. Both are related to fear.

Self-deprecation generates fear directly, and self-importance is really fear hiding underneath ego. Anytime we believe that someone can be of more or less importance than someone else, we are not seeing the world or ourselves clearly, because everyone is equally valuable. No exceptions. When we see the true nature of everyone as equal, and that everyone's opinions, wants, and needs are valuable, then we are anchored in true respect—for ourselves and for others (even those we may disagree with). When you understand and practice this, respect for yourself and others flows naturally from your being.

Let me share an example of how self-respect manifests in our lives, and also see how the traps of self-deprecation and self-importance would look in a specific situation.

A few months ago I began dating someone new, but I came to the realization recently that he was not really available for a deeper, more intimate relationship, and I was. At the beginning of our relationship we were both healing from the end of our previous relationships, so casual outings and occasional get-togethers were what we both needed. Then something shifted inside of me and I recognized I wanted to be fully met as a partner, not just a lover. In the past, I might have ignored this discrepancy in what we both wanted, hoping that he would come around. But I could feel in my being that this would be a disservice to myself. The path to deeply respecting myself was to let him know that I wanted something more, and that because he wasn't available I needed to shift our relationship to being friends rather than lovers. While a part of me didn't want to do this, I felt that doing so would be the most honoring to myself. It was necessary to name my respect for myself and my connection with him so I could focus on creating a great friendship while I opened up elsewhere to what I was seeking in partnership.

Now, my old way of self-importance would say something like, "I can make him love me," or "He should love me; doesn't he realize how lucky he is to have me?" Self-deprecation would say, "He would never love someone like me," or "I'll never get the relationship I want, so I may as well just settle for this." But both of these attitudes are the product of fear rather than respect. With authentic self-respect, you ask yourself, What do I really want in this situation? And when you know the answer to that question, you take the action that respects your choices, no matter where they lead you, and you respect the views of others too. It's a win-win situation. You win because you are authentically respecting your truth. The other wins because they get to know your truth, not your mask. Respecting and sharing your authenticity may feel hard in the short run, but in the long run it will save you and those around you a lot of drama, misunderstanding, and confusion.

As a side note, please remember that there are no right or wrong answers when it comes to deciding what YOU want. Do your best to not judge yourself, compare yourself to others, or feel victimized by the world if your personal preference goes against the wishes of your family, friends, or even societal norms. Judging yourself for feeling a certain way will not bring self-respect, only self-abuse.

From a Warrior Goddess perspective, respect for yourself begins with understanding that honor and dignity for self comes not from trying to be who or what others think you should be, but rather through listening deeply to your innate truth and diligently following your sacred inner guidance and wisdom, no matter where that takes you.

Let's end this section on Warrior Goddess self-respect with a mini credo. Write it down and post it somewhere you can see easily as a daily reminder:

> *As a Warrior Goddess, I will authentically . . .*
>
> Respect my choices,
>
> Respect my body,
>
> Respect my gifts,
>
> Respect my strengths,
>
> Respect my weaknesses,
>
> *And*
>
> Respect my wisdom.
>
> And I will do the same for others.

Now that we have built a new, solid foundation of respect within us, I want to share a secret: respect is only the beginning of authenticity. True authenticity comes from a very unexpected place within you, a place that has no words and no form. In the next chapter, we will befriend the true foundation of all inner authenticity: stillness.

Authenticity: Respect Resources

Gifts

- ◆ When we respect our fears, we become courageous and clear.

- ◆ Respecting others brings inner peace, even when we disagree with them.

- ◆ Authenticity is a journey of inner awakening and a sharing of both your sweet essence and your wacky quirks.

Explorations

CULTIVATING THE INTENT OF RESPECT

Make a written or mental list of the things in your life you are regularly afraid of, from not having enough money to your mother-in-law, getting cancer, or losing your job.

Next, ask yourself, what would respect look like in this situation? What is the essential nature of respect in this situation?

Now, the next time you catch yourself feeling that familiar fear around this topic, try to focus your intent on respect rather than allowing fear to take over and diminish you. Be willing to go under the fear, to the roots beneath the present situation. Don't force. Be a loving guide who directs your "I'm scared" parts toward a bigger view of reality, one where you have options.

NOURISHING SELF-RESPECT

This is another baby steps exercise. First we get the data, and then we explore how we can make little adjustments that will lead to big transformations.

Start by making a list of what you respect about yourself. Start each sentence with "I respect that I . . ." Write without editing.

Here's an example:

> I respect my tenacity.
>
> I respect that I'm a good listener.
>
> I respect my compassion.
>
> I respect my ability to love.
>
> I respect my vision.

Now make a list of places where you are not showing respect for yourself. Start each statement with "I don't show myself respect when I . . ." Again, write without editing or thinking.

Here's an example:

> I don't show myself respect when I say I'll do something and then I don't do it.
>
> I don't show myself respect when I eat foods my body doesn't like.
>
> I don't show myself respect when I put other people's opinions before my own.
>
> I don't show myself respect when I ignore my inner knowing.
>
> I don't show myself respect when I get over-whelmed by my to-do list.

Then name one little thing you can do for each list item that would move you toward self-respect. This doesn't mean you will do things perfectly, but you must be willing to try to take new tiny actions.

Here's an example:

> *Issue*: I don't show myself respect when I say I'll do something and then I don't do it.
>
> *Action*: Today I will focus on celebrating the times when I do follow through with my word.

> *Issue*: I don't show myself respect when I eat foods my body doesn't like.
>
> *Action*: Once a day I'll pick and eat a food that my body likes.

Issue: I don't show myself respect when I put other people's opinions before my own.

Action: I'll keep asking myself what my truth is until I get clear on what is mine and what belongs to other people.

Issue: I don't show myself respect when I ignore my inner knowing.

Action: Today I'll practice respecting all the choices I make, and noticing how each of my choices makes me feel.

Issue: I don't show myself respect when I get overwhelmed by my to-do list.

Action: Today, instead of looking at my huge list, I'll write down two things to do and focus entirely on completing them.

SIX

Authentic Stillness

*In silence, inner energies spontaneously wake up and bring
about the appropriate transformation for every situation.*
—Deepak Chopra

As we learned earlier, the Warrior Goddess Way includes examining our thinking, noticing where it's not in alignment with what's really true for us, and either retraining or redirecting the mind in a way that supports who we really are and how we want to experience life. A key piece in doing this successfully includes giving the mind time to rest, and consciously bringing stillness into your life can help you do exactly that.

Seeing a stillness practice as a tool for anchoring into our authenticity, not to mention a power in itself, can seem antithetical in the modern world. We live in an age where people are constantly on the go, the value of information is judged on how fast it can get to us, and most people will look at you like you're crazy if you suggest they take time to be still. Our daily lives are often dominated by our thinking mind and its desire for "progress."

Most women are super familiar with the part of our mind that berates us, that thinks we should strive to be different than who we authentically are, and that also wants us to believe that critical, comparative thinking (i.e., judging) is indispensable. But when you spend all your time consumed by your thoughts, constantly trying to understand and figure your way through things, the authentic truth of who you are can quickly get lost and distorted, colored in with shades of gray in the form of worry, fear, and uncertainty.

This is not to say that all thinking is bad. I love thinking when it is inspired and creative, or when I need to figure out the tip on a great meal. Thinking is a fabulous gift that has been given to us humans. But when our thinking runs the show—especially when it's filled with judgment and self-doubt rather than peace and joy—then it's time to get still. When we relax into the inner lake of our stillness instead of struggling with the chaotic waves of feeling overwhelmed, worry, and judgment, we learn to listen and act from the still presence of our authentic self rather than the frantic doingness of our busy mind.

I often say that the mind is like a muscle, and if we don't give our muscles a chance to rest, they grow fatigued and weary. Imagine if you went to the gym and worked out your muscles every day to the same extent that you use your mind. Sounds pretty exhausting, doesn't it? Think of stillness as a mental spa that not only leaves you relaxed but also as clear and vibrant as a bubbling creek sparkling over rocks in the sunlight.

The other benefit of implementing a stillness practice is that in addition to improving your mood and creating more peace between your ears, practicing stillness can actually enhance your creativity and increase your performance. Artists of all types will often tell you that their best ideas and inspiration come when they are being still rather than trying to "think everything through." Most of us have experienced the power of stillness in some form or another. For instance, have you ever had the experience of learning a new sport, a new dance, or a foreign language, and when you tried to think about what you were doing or how to do it you got tangled up, but when you let your mind quiet and your body do what it had learned, the right action poured out of you effortlessly?

There is an unexplainable element to stillness that works wonders in the lives of those who have learned to tap into its transformative power. When we get still, quiet the mind, and surrender to the universe, this is often when we have realizations, new ideas, or fresh perspectives, and things otherwise fall into place in an unexplainable way. And while there are no scientific studies to prove how or why this works, anyone who practices bringing stillness into their lives can attest to the truth of it.

Meditations for Women: Four Ways to Quiet Your Mind

In the Native American Toltec tradition, we teach the concept of *mitote*, which is a Nahuatl word used to describe the many voices that chatter loudly in our minds. There isn't a true English language equivalent for this word, so let's go deeper into what the Toltecs meant by this.

If you listen to the conversation that is going on in your head, you'll notice that your internal dialogue is comprised of many different types of voices. There's the judge, the victim, the problem solver, and the heroine, just to name a few, and these various characters have competing narratives on the story of you and your life. Some voices inspire us with their wise song, while others diminish us with their strident demands and loud, clanging fears—and the rest can take a position anywhere in between. But these voices have one thing in common: they all take us out of the present, causing us to cycle old thoughts and memories about the past and then form familiar strategies around imaginary problems in the future (remember, ALL future thinking is imaginary). So instead of being able to be present to what is actually in front of us, our internal dialogue snags our attention in a mess of recycled stories of the past and fabricated fears of the future.

The good news is that the Toltecs, like many other ancient cultures, also had an answer to calming the mental clutter of mitote, and it has proven effective for thousands of years across a variety of spiritual traditions.

Although the word *meditation* can strike anxiety in the hearts of many, meditation is actually a simple and practical act. The traditional point of meditation is to step into the present moment. In their most basic sense, meditation practices are designed to foster inner stillness, and that can be as simple as sitting in silence or moving mindfully. You sit with what is, without judgment, and without trying to change anything. And when you notice that a compelling chain of thoughts has taken you on a journey to someplace besides the present moment, you simply bring your attention back to the here and now.

One of the biggest benefits of meditation is that we learn how to not be so identified with our internal dialogue, or at the very least to not take it so seriously. We begin to recognize that thoughts are simply thoughts, they only exist in our head, and we don't have to believe them. Thoughts are not who we are; rather, we are the aware presence that makes thoughts possible. Meditation helps us experience this truth, and when we remember this throughout our day, it's easier to let go of the thoughts that are causing us suffering.

Authentically connecting with your stillness as a woman often looks and feels different than traditional meditation. Remember, meditation is ultimately not about dogma or rote memorization, so as Warrior Goddesses we need to take the time to discover what works best for us in a stillness/meditation practice.

One of my favorite books on meditation, *Meditation Secrets for Women* by Camille Maureen and Lorin Roche, breaks all the old rules in the best way possible:

> Women need a different kind of meditation approach. Meditation should be joyful, sensuous, engaged, alive. It should be rooted in pleasure. Every woman needs a handful of techniques, not just one. The old rigid time frames, rules about immobility, and devices for blocking feeling deny a woman her basic rights to crave, taste, and experience life as she truly does. Women live right inside the natural rhythms of life—an emotional and physical connection that must be honored and satisfied.

This book paves the way for the radical notion that meditation for women should be authentically *pleasurable*. So if you have been meditating with your judge standing behind you holding a big stick, ready to whack you for any spiritual misdeed, or if you have avoided meditation because it feels too rigid, or if you are ready to explore something new, get ready to throw out the old rule books.

Following are four ways to explore bringing more stillness into your life. As you will see, there are many ways to meditate and dive beneath the noise to tap into your inner silence. If you already have a meditation practice, bravo! Feel free to try any of the methods below or in the resources section at the end of this chapter, as doing so can help you be more aware and bring the stillness of your meditation practice off your cushion and into the rest of your day.

Going forward, I will often use the word "sitting" for uniformity, but this could also include lying down, walking, or otherwise moving your body consciously.

Stillness Meditation

This one is a wonderful place to start for those new to meditation. To begin, find a quiet room inside or a calm and relaxing place outside and simply sit or lie still. Don't worry about any particular sitting position or posture; just find a comfortable position where you can sit or lie quietly and without interruption. For the next five or so minutes, ask yourself, Where is there stillness here? Breathe and get curious about where stillness lives within you. That's it. You can commit to keeping your body as still as possible for the time period you have chosen, or stay connected to your inner stillness while letting your body rock or sway. Your mind may still be busy; just keep bringing your attention back to the stillness within your being. This will teach you how to witness rather than believe your thoughts.

I recommend setting an alarm to go off at the end of the allotted time so you don't have to worry about checking the clock. When the timer beeps, you're done. Again, I suggest starting slow, perhaps even just three to five minutes at first, and gradually build your way up to fifteen or twenty minutes of connecting with your inner stillness.

Listen to Your Inner Silence Meditation

This next meditation is based on one that appears in the *Warrior Goddess Training Companion Workbook* and essentially builds on the foundational practice in the previous example. But this meditation is designed to go a little further, as it can help you deepen your silence within.

To begin, sit comfortably in a quiet room alone or find a quiet place outside. Be sure to turn off the TV, radio, etc., or any other device that is designed to hook your attention. Like the previous exercise, I suggest setting a timer for five minutes and increasing the time as you get more comfortable with meditation. Once the timer is set and you are situated, close your eyes and go inside. In addition to keeping your body still (or moving gently), focus on finding the silence in your mind, which exists in the space between thoughts. As you sit, thoughts will continue to arise, and that's fine. Don't try to force or stop them. Imagine you are in a beautiful, tranquil location, and your thoughts are like diaphanous clouds floating through the sky of your awareness. Bring your awareness to the silent space in between or behind any mental flow and the quiet beauty of your imaginary surroundings.

Finding and noticing this silence is not something you want to try to force, so please don't judge yourself if it seems difficult to pin down at first. Instead, just come back to visualizing a sacred space where you feel completely safe and held, and remind yourself that the silence is within you as well as without. Sit or lie quietly and keep bringing your focus inward. Deepen your breath. Bring one hand to your belly and one hand to your heart. Experience the power of this present moment. Thoughts come and go, but there is an ever-present silence between the thoughts.

Fill the Space Meditation

This next meditation takes an entirely different route to get to the same destination. Instead of sitting or lying down and looking for silence, you will choose a chant or affirmation to say over and over again in your mind. When you give your mind something like this to focus on, you are taking up the brain space your random thoughts would normally occupy. If you can bring your attention fully to the chant or affirmation, you will then begin to feel the silence between each word. Be gentle in coming back to your chosen words over and over again, and let the stillness between the words permeate you.

I like to start my mornings off with chanting, and then take one chant into my day. An affirmation can be one word or a sentence, anything from "peace, peace, peace" to "may I open to all possibilities."

To do this, find a quiet place to sit or lie down comfortably inside or out, set a timer for five minutes, and then begin to speak the chant or affirmation over and over in your mind, or, even better, out loud. Be present with each word, giving it your complete attention. If you notice the mind getting lost in a chain of thought, bring your attention back to your words. Gradually work your way up to chanting for twenty minutes over time.

This meditation is also a great one to take with you. You can repeat your chant or affirmation while you walk, while driving to work, or anyplace you want to shift the energy of your mind. The key is to stay present with and bring the calm feeling of your chant or affirmation into your body, so you are experiencing the quality of the words rather than just thinking them.

Time in Nature: A Walking Meditation

This mediation is also similar to one that appears in the *Warrior Goddess Training Companion Workbook*, but we go deeper here.

The wild is a great teacher of stillness. Even though there may be birds chirping, leaves crackling underfoot, and wind whistling through the trees, the silence held in nature is tangible.

The first step of this meditation is to get outside in a nearby forest, a local park, or even your own backyard. Some people prefer the desert, others the beach. Anyplace you can feel a connection to the natural world will work fine, although typically the more distant from civilization, the better.

Once you find a quiet place, take a mental step into the present moment. Be here, now. For the next few minutes, make an inner commitment to leaving all your mental noise behind in the "civilized" world. Next, feel your feet grounded in the earth, and know the Mother is beneath you and that all around you is family. As you look at your surroundings, imagine that along with all the humans on the planet, every tree, flower, rock, mountain, skyscraper, sidewalk, insect, four-legged animal, and winged animal is your brother and sister. You are never alone, and you are never without guidance. Everything you see is here to support you.

Now begin to walk, and be conscious of each step you take. Let it keep you grounded in the present moment. So many times we walk while our minds are someplace else (we're on the phone, thinking about what we have planned for the evening, etc.). But on this walk, your only purpose is to walk consciously, staying aware of your present surroundings. Slow down and use all of your senses. With each step, feel your feet touching the ground. Notice the wind against your skin and the touch of your clothing. Smell the air. Widen your vision and soften your gaze so you take in as much of your surroundings as possible, without fixating on any one thing. Let your ears take in all the different sounds around you: birds, car doors slamming, twigs cracking, your breath. Let all the sensations wash through you as life's flow. There is nothing to fix or change.

Walk for at least ten minutes in this way, and gradually work your way up to longer periods. When you notice your mind has strayed into what you have planned for tomorrow or what happened yesterday, don't beat yourself up; instead, gently steer your mind back to an awareness of your surroundings by focusing on each step you take.

In addition to these four meditation exercises, I encourage you to explore the many other traditions of meditation that exist in the world, and to especially give yourself permission to create meditations that will serve where you are now. You don't have to follow any rules. Let your wisdom guide you in how to connect to your authentic stillness. For example, recently I've been waking up and lying in bed for my meditation practice. Each morning, wrapped in the comfort of my purple flannel sheets, I breathe into my full body and feel the pleasure of being alive. Then I roll over and watch the wind in the leaves of the tree outside my bedroom window. When I get up, I feel happy and clear, and I'm more easily able to witness my thoughts and make better choices of where I want to put my attention.

There are so many different ways to meditate, but most have one thing in common: they invite more peace and clarity into our lives. As we move into stillness, we also begin to learn how the mind thinks, and one area you might notice needs adjustment is the way you ask questions.

Questions Can Create Noise or Bring Stillness

If you haven't noticed, the mind loves to ask questions! This is something that has been acknowledged in spiritual traditions from around the world. In Hinduism, the mind's desire "to know" is identified as one of its five primary attributes. In the Western world, many of the principles of philosophy, law, and government are built on what's called the Socratic method, or a process of perfecting one's reasoning skills through asking questions. But what Western culture has forgotten is that the logical, linear mind is not where we find all our answers. More importantly, the way the mind often asks questions can actually hinder us from finding the truth that we seek.

For instance, have you ever said to yourself something like, "Why is this happening to me?" "What did I do to deserve this?" or "Why can't I just be happy?"

As you may already notice, questions phrased like the ones above often create fear and anxiety that can drain our energy, scatter our attention, and keep us stuck. No authentic answer can arise, because implicit in the question is a sense of blame, punishment, or victimhood. These questions subtly carry negative emotions that are directed at ourselves, at another, or even at life itself. The mind loves asking loaded questions like these, and then the mitote, or the multiple voices in our head, love to shout out a variety of unhelpful answers.

At my workshops, I have women feel into a place they have been struggling and then find the main question they have been asking themselves around that topic. Let's look at some common questions I've heard women share at these gatherings. Perhaps you will recognize a few:

- Why don't I have enough time?

- Why is this happening to me?

- Why doesn't he/she like me?

- Why can't I find the love that I need?

- What is wrong with me?

- What did I do to deserve this?

- Why do I always end up in this type of relation-
  ship/situation?

Before we go further, I want to point out that depending on the energy you put behind them, the questions in this
list can be helpful, but oftentimes that is the exception rather
than the rule. In other words, you could ask yourself, "Why
do I *always* procrastinate?" in a bitter, frustrated, accusatory
way, or you could ask yourself the same question from a place
of curiosity and genuine wonder: "Why do I always procrastinate?" The important thing is to notice the questions you're
asking yourself and the energy they generate in the process.

For most of the women in my workshops, asking questions like the ones in this list are part of the problem, because
they are usually tainted with the negative emotions of guilt,
blame, and fear. Questions phrased like the ones on that list
most often presuppose that there is something wrong with us,
with another, or with the world. Because these questions are
based in the energy of fear and perpetuate the false belief that
we are not enough, no helpful answer can come from putting
them this way.

So what's the Warrior Goddess solution? Ask better questions, and go into the stillness!

This can be a difficult lesson to understand and implement at first, as the very nature of asking questions from a place of stillness is hard to express in words, but the spirit of this process involves asking new types of questions that come from your authentic curiosity—ones that you feel into, rather than try to answer with your logical or thinking mind. The difference can be found in the energy of the inquiry. When we bring our attention to creating questions from stillness, we tap into a deeper sense of inquisitiveness that is based in unconditional love and infinite choice, and the answers that arise from this place strengthen our innate connection to Spirit and foster the growth of our sacred creativity and feminine depth.

For the most important questions, the answers you seek can't be found in the logical and linear gyrations of the mind, but rather in the stillness and mystery that are the source of all life. Our grandmothers' grandmothers knew this, as did all those who honored the ancient feminine way of knowing.

When our most intimate questions come exclusively from the dryness of our logical mind, we don't take into account the multilayered heart and soul of our being. If we make choices only from what our mind thinks must be logically true, we cut ourselves off from our emotional body, which leaves us numb and robotic. For some questions, we don't want to ask them from the place of the mind—instead we incubate them in the dark womb of our being and let the answers be birthed within us.

Let's rewrite the questions above from a place of stillness to better see what I mean.

- "Why don't I have enough time?" becomes "What actions can I take to create more space in my life?"

- "Why is this happening to me?" becomes "What do I want to change in my life?"

- "Why doesn't he/she like me?" becomes "Do I like me?"

- "Why can't I find the love that I need?" becomes "How can I give myself the love that I need?"

- "What is wrong with me?" becomes "What do I need to become aware of?"

- "What did I do to deserve this?" becomes "What am I grateful for?"

- "Why do I always end up in this type of relationship/situation?" becomes "What do I want to deeply engage with at this time of my life?"

Asking questions with the right energy, which means from a place of openness, curiosity, and unconditional self-love, prepares you to receiving authentic answers from stillness. The answers you get from the deep well of connection within you will be far better than those that come from the thinking mind. Incubate your questions in the dark stillness. Go beneath your thoughts to the spacious, patient, primordial womb of the goddess, so the answers become an experience born within you rather than a disembodied thought. This is the Warrior Goddess Way of asking questions, and we will practice this further in the explorations section at the end of this chapter.

Silence as a Gateway to Stillness

Practicing silence is another tool that can help you get in touch with your inner stillness. In some cases it can take a little while, as it did with me.

Many years ago, when I was apprenticing with don Miguel Ruiz, I decided to enter a time of silence. I wanted to get quiet, so I made the decision to "fast" for forty days from speaking and from external stimulation. While I still worked and interacted with the world, I gave up a lot of things: TV, radio, Internet, reading material, words. I carried a notepad with me wherever I went, and when people would talk to me I would hold up a note that said "I am in silence."

For the first thirty days I battled with my mind. There was no peace, only my disaster mind trying to get my attention by becoming increasingly louder and more obnoxious. I stayed committed to my silence even though it seemed I was a hopeless cause for ever quieting my mind.

And then one day I noticed something fascinating.

I was walking with someone as they talked to me about a problem they were having. At the end of the conversation they looked at me and said, "Thank you so much for your help. I feel so much better." Which was great, except I hadn't said a word. And I realized my mind had been very still during our walk.

I puzzled about this for a few days.

Then it happened again. I found people genuinely loved being around me in my silence, and they found answers to their questions and insights just by being in a one-way conversation with me. As someone who felt that she had to always have the right answers and had spent a lot of time verbally helping people, this was very strange indeed.

But I recognized that in my extended silence I had finally learned to fully, completely show up for people and to be internally still. There was no trying to figure out what they needed to hear, plan what I would say next, or coming up with a story of my own to match their story. I was mentally still, and people felt it.

While spending forty days in silence may not be realistic or necessary for you, I would encourage you to try to spend some time simply being quiet throughout your day. Use this time to listen to your heart instead of trying to find the answers in your head. Let the stillness bring your internal wisdom up from the depths, and let this silent wisdom spill out to touch everyone around you. And take it from someone who knows: being silent can be very difficult at first, as the mind needs time to adjust and unwind, but conscious silence can be a wonderful step in the direction of finding you inner stillness.

Stillness in Action

I am often asked about stillness and its effect in the "real world." In other words, people often agree that getting quiet is helpful in a retreat setting, but they want to know the practical value it has in everyday situations. While it's only the mind that questions the value of stillness, let's satisfy the mind's curiosity by recounting an experience I had in an emergency situation that bountifully demonstrates the power of taking action from stillness.

On a break from a retreat in Mexico, my co-facilitator, Will Taegel, and I were talking when I thought I heard what sounded like someone calling out in distress. At first I wasn't sure where the sound had come from or even what it was, but when I heard it again, we both got up and walked toward the source—the hallway upstairs. "We need help! Christine has fallen!"

Christine was lying on the ground, obviously in pain but completely calm. Two women gathered around her, and as Will and I walked up, one of the women said, "She broke her wrist."

Before Christine's hand swelled any more, Will started to pull her ring off.

"Do you need lotion?" someone asked.

"Yes," Will said.

"Here is some," someone else said. The ring came off easily and was handed to someone for safekeeping.

"We need a magazine to make a splint," someone said calmly.

"I'll get one," I heard myself say. I turned around and headed down the stairs, wondering where I was going to find a magazine. I headed out the front door and toward the house I was staying at, and then I felt a *no* in my body. I stopped. Listened. Turned around and walked toward the kitchen. My mind was a little puzzled, but my body felt clear. Then I looked down and saw a small stack of magazines I had never noticed before. I grabbed two and headed back up the stairs.

On the way back up to Christine, I realized we were going to need a scarf to tie the splint. I started trying to figure out where to find a scarf, and a thought popped into my head: *I should look in my room.* I turned that way but felt a clear urge to head up the stairs, back toward Christine. So I trusted my silent instinct and turned back around. My mind became quiet again. On the staircase I passed my friend Shiila, who I saw was wearing the perfect scarf.

"Can I borrow your scarf?" I asked her.

"Yes!" she replied as she pulled it off her neck.

My entire trip was under two minutes. I'd found two things I urgently needed by walking right to them—no searching required. Something other than my rational mind was definitely at work.

The entire rest of that day and the next, from getting Christine down the stairs to the doctor to getting her on a flight home, continued to unfold in this way. There was no drama, no story, no fear. There was simply a community in action, listening for guidance, letting stillness lead. Beautiful.

On the deepest level, the more you cultivate stillness in your life, the more you realize it's who you actually are. Even in the most chaotic and stressful situations, stillness is there to assist you if you can tap into it. When we get still and quiet our mind, things often fall into place in a most magical, unexplainable way.

And now, in our final chapter in the authenticity section, we'll learn how to actively turn on five often underutilized aspects of our being to bring us into the most sacred, authentic place of all: pure, conscious awareness.

Authenticity: Stillness Resources

Gifts

- True authenticity is not just about action, but blossoms naturally from the roots of your stillness.

- As a woman, it is vital for you to give yourself permission to find or create a meditation/stillness practice that works for you.

- Learn to rewrite your questions so they carry you into the depth of your silence rather than getting you stuck in the worry of your mind.

Explorations

STILLNESS IN THE IN-BETWEEN PLACES

Get habituated to taking breaks during the day to sink into silence: when going to the bathroom, while eating, in between meetings or clients. Instead of running from thing to thing, thinking all the time, breathe into your feet. Notice the colors around you. Slow down. Walk more slowly between places. Reconnect with silence consciously.

What happens if you ride in the car without the radio on? Or refrain from speaking unnecessarily in a conversation? Practicing silence in these little ways can help you slow down and move into stillness.

BIRTHING NEW QUESTIONS

Get quiet for a moment, and listen within for a question you have asked yourself recently that does not serve you. It may be one from the list provided earlier in the chapter, or it may be another one.

Take a moment and write the question down, or say it out loud. Notice how it makes you feel. If you want to get the full experience, walk around and act your question out while stating it over and over again. For example, you might ask, "Why does this always happen to me?" while moping and pouting with slouched shoulders and a protruding lip. Pause, take a breath, and scan your body to see how the question drains or scatters your energy.

Now, put one hand on your belly and the other hand on your heart. Breathe into both hands and say hello to yourself. Get quiet. Exhale out the old question. Bless it, and thank it for trying to keep you safe or helping you try to make sense of the world. Now, ask yourself the new question. Hold your head up, close your eyes, and get still. You are genuinely open to finding out and welcoming the answer. For example, you might ask, "What do I want to change in my life?".

Now for the stillness magic: Do not try to answer this new question. Don't let your mind grab hold of it and try to make sense of it and figure it out! Drop into your belly, into the dark cave of your womb. Listen. Let the answers arise spontaneously, over time. Swaddle the question in stillness and let it germinate in the dark soil within. The answers that ultimately sprout from your inner goddess may surprise you.

SANCTUARY MEDITATION

I learned this beautiful meditation-visualization from one of my first teachers, Cerridwen Fallingstar. I've been doing it regularly for over two decades. The more you meditate on your inner sanctuary, the more it cultivates a safe haven of stillness within you.

Before you start this meditation, make sure you have twenty minutes of undisturbed time. Turn your phone off, close the door, make boundaries.

Imagine yourself someplace beautiful in nature. It may be someplace you've been many times, or someplace you've seen pictures of or only dreamt about. In your imagination you can go anywhere.

Take your time walking around and getting to know this area. Let yourself relax and explore this nourishing place.

When you are ready, look for a house or an enclosed structure that feels safe and sweet. This is your sanctuary, a place you can retreat to and close the door. You can make it a cabin in the woods, or a temple on the beach, or a glass building on a mountainside; be creative! Walk around the building and get to know it. How big is it? How is it hidden from the world so it is just for you? Is there a garden, or forest, or desert surrounding it?

Once you enter, use your imagination to decorate your sanctuary however you want. What would soothe and help you feel completely at home here? Create a magical space where you can go inside, protected from the world, held in your bubble of the sacred.

Once a day for the next week, visit your sanctuary. Keep building in details. While you are there, imagine that the moment you walk through the door you let go of your worldly concerns. Sit in the center of your sanctuary and tap into your stillness. Your sanctuary is the center of your heart, the place of inner peace that resides within you. By giving it form in your mind's eye, you will be able to rest into being held in silence and spaciousness.

You can get a free copy of this meditation by visiting www.heatherashamara.com.

SEVEN

Authentic Awareness

When we really start to take a look at who we think we are, we become very grace prone. We start to see that while we may have various thoughts, beliefs, and identities, they do not individually or collectively tell us who we are. . . . It is actually astounding how completely we humans define ourselves by the content of our minds, feelings, and history.
—Adyashanti

Have you ever noticed that you often look simply to confirm what you already think you will see? Or that you often listen to confirm what you expect you will hear? When we do this, we live our lives based on what we *think* we will experience rather than actually having an experience, fresh and new in the present moment. As a result, things rarely change for us, as we more than likely will get what we are already expecting. Even when something else is present, we often can't see it because we aren't open to the possibility of its existence. It's like eating porridge at every meal because it is familiar and ignoring the glorious buffet overflowing with delicious, mouthwatering foods that surrounds you.

I call this the trap of living from the mind rather than living from the heart. When we live without being conscious of what's happening in the present moment, our mind takes over, and our thoughts end up dictating—and therefore limiting—our experience.

Once you start paying attention to the thoughts that arise in your field of consciousness, there is something else you will notice: your thoughts are rarely about the present moment. As women, we often define ourselves and the world around us from the well-trodden past, which doesn't allow us to be in vibrancy of the ever-changing present. The mind spends much of its time worrying about the past or fretting about the future, and in the process you miss the only life that ever happens: the moment you are living in right now.

Noticing these habits of the mind—where your thoughts and expectations prejudge and predetermine your experience, or constantly whisk your attention away from the present and into the future or the past—shows you the areas where your attention needs some refocusing. What you need to free your mind from its crowded jail of limited perception is already within you: the vastness of your true self, your awareness.

Developing a practice of awareness is advocated in the mystical aspects of every major religious and spiritual tradition, and because different traditions define awareness in different ways, let's take a moment to explain exactly how we are going to use awareness as part of the Warrior Goddess Way.

Awareness is the art of being fully present, acutely cognizant of what is happening in *this* moment, both within and without. In other words, you simultaneously observe what is happening in the exterior world and witness your inner reaction to it.

When you are in touch with what is happening in the present moment, you can see things as they actually are rather than how the mind *thinks* they should be. When you are focused on experiencing your surroundings, it's much harder for the mind to hook your attention with all its reveling in drama, doubt, and dysfunction.

In addition to this outer watching, the practice of awareness means you also watch your internal reactions to this exterior stimulus, because in doing so you will learn more about yourself. In this way, awareness is the key to practicing all the other tools on the Warrior Goddess path, because the first step to changing anything is to become aware of the need for change.

Many women I work with have never heard of awareness as a practice, much less tried it. But even if you are already on board and practicing awareness, it's something you can always go deeper with, and this chapter will be devoted to helping you do exactly that. Best of all, the rest of this chapter is devoted to creating an Awareness practice using five powerful means that you likely have already: your senses.

Your Senses: A Gateway to Awareness

Each sense, when used consciously, helps you to come fully into the awareness of the present, which is the only place where you can be authentic. Your senses can bring you back into the truth of this moment—the physical reality of now, rather than thinking about what you wish or think should be. It is only here, in this moment and this time, that you can release the mistakes and regrets of the past as well as the worries and fears of the future.

It's amazing how when we make that tiny shift from *thinking* about the past and future or trying to figure out who we are supposed to be to fully living in the present moment *from our hearts* that we bring more radiance to our being and sparkle to our eyes. As the Russian mystic and philosopher G. I.

Gurdjieff wrote, "It is only by grounding our awareness in the living sensation of our bodies that the 'I Am,' our real presence, can awaken."

As we move through each of the five senses, one at a time, from sight to sound, smell to taste, and then to touch, I invite you to read and contemplate the five sections with the spirit of openness, letting go of any expectations. Release what you think you know about your senses and how they are used. Look at the power of your senses as if you were a child—with awe and playfulness. Let yourself drink in all the information and use the teachings to increase your awareness of all of your senses, a little bit at a time. As you shed your familiar fixation on the ghosts of the past and future you'll discover the radiant beauty of this moment, and your authenticity will naturally shine from the center of an embodied now.

Sight

Our sense of sight comes from light entering our eyes, but it is not only the organ of our eyes that creates sight; our brain ultimately decides how we perceive the world. When we unconsciously use our sight, we see the world through our own mental filters and distortions, and our perception of events is colored by the lens of our fears and regrets.

Warrior Goddesses can learn to use their eyes as mirrors, taking in what is and cleaning the distortions of our past experiences. Wise use of sight comes through strengthening our witness-self, so we simultaneously see both the world and our inner reaction to it. Doing so creates the spaciousness within so we can see beyond our filters and choose our subsequent response, rather than react based on the conditioning of our past.

When we use our eyesight mindfully, we see what is with awareness, and this brings us into a state of absolute choice in both our response and in our state of being.

For example, one day I was walking by the river that runs through downtown Austin when I noticed a small pile of trash. After I picked up the trash and put it in a nearby trash can I mused at how different my perception is nowadays. In the past I would have seen the trash and started judging the individual who left the trash there, and then gone on to judge all Americans for how much they litter (*The trash can was* right there! *What is wrong with people!?*), and then berate all humans for how careless and disrespectful they are to Mother Earth. I would have held myself as more "evolved" than whoever left this trash, and I would have felt self-righteous, angry, and disheartened all at the same time. I would have created a narrative that would elevate my emotions and discolor my experience of the present moment.

All from a few pieces of trash.

Acting from pure perception without the judgment, story, or filter of "good" or "bad," what actually happened was this: I saw the trash, I admired the bright red of the coke bottle, and I chose to bend down, pick it up, and put it in the trash can.

If we see old bottles and newspapers that have been discarded on the side of the road, we can simply see what is: old bottles and newspapers. Period. Side of the road. Period. Or we can see these items as "bad," which carries with it a condemnation from the mind and creates a whole story of the laziness of humans and the destruction of civilization.

When you see the world from the clarity of truth without the story, what happens next is miraculous: you can take action on what you see from a place of choice rather than a conditioned response. Remember, the trash is the trash, whether you are hating it, loving it, or neutral about it.

People sometimes tell me they worry that if they didn't have the judgment toward "bad" things they see in the world—trash, child prostitution, starvation, animal abuse, climate change—that nothing would ever change and we would just walk through our lives mindlessly as the world goes to hell in a handbasket. What I've found is the opposite. Sitting in these negative emotions doesn't foster lasting positive change. When we see what is with clarity and are moved by the inspiration of our heart instead of the fear and judgment of our mind, we are actually much more effective, creative, and deliberate in our actions.

For instance, without the negative emotions of anger and judgment when you see the trash, you may be inspired to pick up all the trash in the park that you see that day, or start a monthly Pick Up the Trash Day with your friends, or even start an organization dedicated to educating people about caring for the environment. All of these possibilities are far more likely to arise from a place positive inspiration rather than the negative emotions of anger or judgment.

SEEING EXERCISE

Notice how the mind constantly wants to label everything it sees: chair, book, paper, table, house, spouse, etc. This habit of immediately labeling everything that enters our field of vision has the negative effect of closing off the beauty of the present moment. When the mind thinks it knows something, it stops looking and perceiving. The mind's judgments about these labels follows next: trash = bad; chair = I like that one; table = useful.

In this exercise, I want you to practice perceiving the world around you from your heart, without adding the filters of your mind and past experiences. The first step is to try not to label the things you see. You see a chair—but is that really what it is? Or is that just what we call it? Really look. See the crazy variety of colors in the world. Notice the shapes of objects in front of you. See your family or coworkers with the eyes of a newborn, as if you have never met them before. Look at yourself in the mirror as if you are seeing a human for the first time. Let your heart open your eyes.

Next, notice the stories that are attached to what you see, and practice witnessing them with your inner eyes rather than taking them as the truth. Is what you are seeing really true? Is there another angle of perception that would change everything?

For example, I can see someone else's frown as I'm talking, and instead of adding a caption to the picture: "They are frowning because they don't like me," I can simply notice the frown and stay present with our conversation. Or I can say, "You have a frown on your face. What are you thinking about?" And get more information.

Instead of automatically (and usually incorrectly) filling in the blanks when you see something, notice what past experiences you are projecting into the present moment and the story you are creating as a result. Seeing without immediately labeling or adding a narrative allows you to freely choose your actions in the present moment.

Sound

Every day our ears hear thousands of sounds emanating from all around us, while our mind filters "what is relevant" and pays attention to only that. The voices from other tables in a coffee shop, the freeway noise outside our office, the hum of the refrigerator all seem to disappear.

As humans, we have a phenomenal capacity to accept or reject the flow of sense information around us, but that's not always the case with the internal sounds. As Warrior Goddesses of awareness, the goal is to capture this natural quality of discernment that we have with external noises and use it skillfully to free ourselves from the internal voices of self-abuse and self-judgment.

One the biggest impediments to living and being in joy comes when we are tuned in to the distracting, nagging drip of our judgments and fears. When we get hooked into listening to these negative voices, we hear only the warnings of limitations and criticism, which drown out the sounds of our inner wisdom.

The internal and external are related, as what you hear on the inside is reflected in the tenor and pitch of the voices you choose to listen to on the outside. For example, imagine you are in a room with a hundred people. Ninety-nine of them are telling you how wonderful you are, but one person is saying, "You are a fraud. You are not a good person. You are unlovable." What would hook your attention? Many women I know will literally ignore the majority of blessings and hone in on the voice of negativity because it is so familiar.

And on the other hand, we can also live in a fantasy and only hear the exact things we want to and filter out what we don't want to be reality. Women do this especially in situations like dating. "But he told me he loved me!" my friend said to me, devastated that the man she was seeing suddenly stopped calling her after a couple of weeks. As we talked further, it turned out he had said those words once in the throes of lovemaking but had repeated to her over and over that he was not interested in an intimate relationship. But she only wanted to hear that he wanted to be with her, so she ignored what she didn't want to hear and grabbed on to a scrap of evidence to prove the reality she was hoping for.

Can you notice which external voices stick and which roll off you? Do you grab criticism but filter out compliments? Do you only hear what you want to hear and ignore anything else?

Bringing awareness to the inner and outer voices we choose to listen to allows us to rewire our internal and external hearing to see the benefits of the present moment and the creative possibilities of the future and release any voices that are keeping us chained to the past.

Oftentimes, voices get stuck in our head that berate, criticize, or negate our worth. Sometimes the voices are from something painful that someone in our past actually said to us that we continue to repeat. Sometimes the voices are from the fictional stories of our own inner judge.

Learning to use your hearing in a new way means first opening up your awareness to take everything in, then using your being's ninja-like listening filter to adjust what you are taking in and what you are filtering out.

HEARING EXERCISE

Open up your auditory perception by listening to the birds, the wind, the cars, the barking dog, the sounds of your clothing. Listen. Take it all in. Practice this deep listening at your lunch breaks, as you walk down the hall to the bathroom, at your kid's soccer game. Notice how the mind deems so many of these sounds as unimportant, yet maintains the supremacy of its own voice, as if it's constantly saying, "*Psst!* I have something important to tell you, and you need to be very afraid, or worried, or excited!" Who decided that the voices of your mind were more important than the external sounds of the present moment? The mind did, of course. But the truth is that listening to the sounds of the moment can be far more beneficial to your being than listening to the negative voices of fear, doubt, and judgment that the mind declares are so important. The next time you notice a continual stream of worrisome, judgmental thoughts, use this as a chance to listen to what's happening around you instead.

Once you are able to witness the variety of sounds around you, tune back in to your inner voices. You'll notice there is not just one voice, but many. This is what the Toltecs call the mitote that I explained earlier or the myriad of voices in your mind that are clambering for attention.

For this exercise, I want you to listen to these voices as if you were listening to the television or a conversation at the lunch table next to you. Be curious about what the themes are, which voices are the loudest, and which ones get drowned out. Write down anything you notice from your listening. Then begin to tune in to the voices that you want to guide you, and imagine turning down the volume of the voices that don't serve you. Be patient as you do this massive rewiring of which voices you choose to listen to and which ones you want to diminish. Becoming aware of the voices is the first step.

Note: Rather than trying to shut down any of the voices out of anger or frustration, I tend to say to them, "Wow, you are being so good at judging!" or "I hear that you want to throw a temper tantrum right now." And then from that place of witness I choose where I want to put my attention. Be compassionate but firm with yourself, and take back your power to listen and witness rather than believing everything you hear between and beyond your ears.

Taste

Our sense of taste is a major doorway to living in the present, and a great key for Warrior Goddesses to open the lock on habitual disconnection and distraction. When we stop to taste our food fully, to savor the flavors and textures, we slow down and reconnect with the pleasure of being alive.

So many women struggle with food and body image, which I believe is tied to not letting ourselves truly receive the sweetness of life. We substitute truly taking in and digesting the simple joys for the fleeting satisfaction of a cookie or the kick of a latte. Don't get me wrong—I love a good cookie! But we want to be honest about where we are out of balance with what we are putting in our mouths, and why. For instance, do you usually taste your food with awareness? Are you listening to the authentic messages from your body about what it prefers?

You honor your Warrior Goddess self when you take the time to learn what best serves *your* body. Let go of all the information you've read about what is good and what is bad and actually ask the one true expert: you. Books are great for reference, but the only truly reliable source for information about your body comes from the one who is in it!

Sometimes your taste buds, and your body, get confused about what is good for you. If you've been eating a lot of sugar and salt, you can become accustomed to that and think you prefer junk food to fresh fruits and vegetables. Similarly, if you've gotten used to tolerating low-quality relationships in your life, your body can get used to that too. Use your awareness to wean yourself off nonnutritious filler foods and toxic relationships.

Make a commitment to eat one meal a day (or at least one meal a week) with your full awareness. Pick foods you know your body (not just your mouth or mind!) will appreciate. Chew each bite, savoring the taste. Eat until you are about two-thirds full, then stop.

Notice how the food you've eaten interacts with your body as it moves through your digestive tract. Do you feel overly full? Does your stomach cramp? Does your energy dip after you eat? Do you get constipated? Your body is constantly talking to you about what it does and doesn't like. Imagine your sense of taste is linked to your entire digestive tract, and listen to what taste your body likes.

Here is a big challenge: I invite you to cut sugar out of your diet for a month. I know, crazy! But I guarantee that after the first week or so your taste buds will come alive. Carrots, strawberries, even cooked onions will taste super sweet and decadent. And your body will be so much happier. There are many wonderful books that explain the benefits of this diet and how to wean yourself from sugar in a good way. I invite you to check out the Free Stuff section at www.heatherashamara.com for more information and recipes.

Smell

Our sense of smell brings in the scents of life, is directly tied to taste, and forms a strong pathway to memories. Nothing opens us more than a smell we love, and few things can make us recoil as quickly as a smell we dislike. Just take a whiff. Cinnamon buns fresh out of the oven. Coffee. Lemon Pledge. Dog poop on your shoe. Linked to these images are not only the smell, but also some experience you have had with them.

Here are mine: my ex and his childlike glee when eating a good cinnamon bun. Coffee shops and writing late into the night. My grandmother's house on Maple Street in Lynn, Massachusetts. Making smelly tracks across the porch after I unknowingly stepped in a squishy pile.

Of all the myriad smells in the world, some are pleasant and some are unpleasant. We lean happily toward roses and freshly baked bread, while we lean quickly away from stinky garbage and exhaust fumes. The Warrior Goddess learns to lean toward all smells and experiences, bringing her awareness to all manifestations of the divine flow, releasing the labels of "good" and "bad," and embracing the wisdom of all.

Here is a wise quote from Seng-ts'an, a Chinese Buddhist teacher who lived in the fifth century AD:

> The Great Way is not difficult for those who have no preferences. When love and hate are both absent everything becomes clear and undisguised. Make the smallest distinction, however, and heaven and earth are set infinitely apart.

Smell is an ever-present tool we can use to gently dissolve preferences, bring clarity, and dance down the Warrior Goddess Way with joy for both the sweet and the stink of life. Let's look at how this can be done in the following exercise.

SMELLING EXERCISE

The next time you notice a smell you would normally recoil from, practice opening to it without judgment. Simply be aware of it. Relax your face, soften your body, and breathe. Nothing happens next. Say to yourself, "This is just a smell."

Be grateful for your sense of smell. Keep releasing "bad," "icky," "nasty," "ugh." This is a smell. Relax your shoulders. Notice how the smell passes.

This simple practice can be transferred to help you release other preferences and make your days inwardly sweeter. For instance, when in traffic, release "bad," "frustrating," and "wrong." This is just traffic. Relax your neck. Breathe. When you can't find your favorite product at a store, substitute, and see if you can simply be with what is. Preferences are fun to celebrate when they are met, and this practice will help you not suffer if your preferences are not met.

Note: For those of you who have a history of being caretakers and people pleasers, remember that you first have to own your own personal preferences before you start removing them in earnest. So if you do not know what your preferences are because you've always bowed down to other people's wants, I invite you to start naming what you like and what you don't like, just for you. This will define your boundaries as separate from others. Then, once you have a sense of self-identity, you can practice letting go of "like" and "dislike."

Touch

Touching with awareness is another way to bring us into the present moment. It gets us out of our heads and into our bodies, and it relaxes our nervous system. When we take in and receive all kinds of touch—our hand on our belly in reassurance, the kiss of the wind on our cheek, the solid, rough bark of a tree we are leaning against, a hug from a friend—we take in the pleasure that connects us to all creation, the touch of the Goddess manifest.

Very few of us get enough human touch. When I first moved to Thailand as a kid, I remember being amazed to see that people always walked hand in hand with their friends. The Thais touched each other with ease and kindness. When I moved to the States, it felt like there was a huge, unbreachable touch gulf between friends—unless you were being sexual with them.

When I met my friend Jesikah, who coincidentally also spent time as a kid in Southeast Asia, I loved how she would touch every person she interacted with in the most natural way. It never felt awkward or invasive; it was always a friendly, loving connection. I wished I had the same gift of healing, connecting touch that she did. Eventually, I released my own shyness and fear of being rejected and learned to bring loving touch into my conversations.

Today, I consciously touch people as often as feels good. Some people don't like to be touched, and of course that is to be respected, no questions asked. But many people crave the simple human gift of a hand on the arm; a kiss on the cheek; or a good, warm hug. Also play with consciously touching other pleasurable things: petting animals, leaning your body up against trees, resting your cheek on the cool marble of a kitchen counter. Let your aware, mindful touch create more authentic, present communion with life: people, plants, animals, minerals, and more.

TOUCHING EXERCISE

Start with learning how to touch your body with your full presence. Bring your hands together, feeling the pleasure of touching them gently, feeling skin against skin, noticing the sensitivity of your fingers and palms interacting. If you witness yourself getting into your head, close your eyes. Cup your cheeks in your hands, resting into your touch. Receive. Bring your hands to anyplace you feel stiffness or pain in your body and send yourself loving-kindness. In the shower, slow down and let your hands touch and honor each part of your body, from toes to scalp.

Now let nature touch you. Open to the wind, to the grass beneath your feet (take those shoes off for a minute!) and to the soft nose of your dog. Take in the pleasure of touch. Let it expand your perceptions and soothe your animal self. So much of what we are craving is available in a thousand little ways.

Then bring your touch to your closest friends. Put a gentle hand on their arm when you are talking. Take someone's hand when you are walking with them. Give hugs freely. You will be amazed at how some people will open up to you and how some of your friendships will become deeper when you consciously bring more touch into your interactions.

Releasing Definitions, Embracing Now

By releasing all the old definitions of who you are and living through your five senses, you connect with the immense gifts that each sense provides. Use your Warrior Goddess mojo to focus on them one at a time, making the most of every sense so you can make contact with the majesty of your inner temple and touch the wide-open mystery that surrounds you.

With this new base of sacred awareness you will find yourself naturally more and more authentic, present, and joyful. Don't fall asleep to the wonders of your senses; they are here to help you be you fully!

From this place of authentic awareness, let's travel into the world of saying YES, and learn how this one word is your passport to freedom.

Authenticity: Awareness Resources
Gifts

- Without realizing it, we often use our senses to look and listen for what we already know.

- Awareness frees us of the weight of past thinking and the burden of future worry by bringing our attention to learn and engage from our current inner and outer experiences.

- Our five senses are ever-present tools to bring us back to our authentic, in-the-now, experiencing self.

Exploration

CELEBRATING OUR SENSES

A chapter on awareness is by definition an exploration in and of itself. I invite you to reread and contemplate the section on the five senses, but this time do a different sense each day for five days. Practice disconnecting each sense from your thinking and connecting your sacred sight, touch, taste, smell, and hearing to your heart. Spend the whole day focusing on your awareness through one particular sense. Invite in each of your senses as a teacher bringing you new wisdom and guidance.

Part Three

YES!

Yes! is about celebrating. Everything. All the time. And that is one serious art that's not for the faint of heart. Most of us love to celebrate our successes, but what I'm talking about is celebrating even your greatest losses. That means looking for the gift in every situation, even when something doesn't go your way. Finding joy in your grief. Enthusiastically embracing your shadow. High-fiving yourself when you screw up. And then bringing 100 percent of yourself to the next action.

Before we begin the final chapters of the Warrior Goddess Way, I want to take a moment to introduce you to the radical Warrior Goddess practice that will serve as the touchstone for the remainder of this book: the art of learning to love it all. While this can sometimes be just as difficult as it sounds, the first step begins with watching your mind, seeing any nos that arise there, and working toward replacing them with yeses.

We can all think of situations where we say no in both big and little ways. The no to traffic. The no to rain. The no to those crinkly wrinkles around your eyes. The no to the end of a relationship you don't want to end. The no to cancer. And so on. But what all these things have in common is that when they occur, they do so whether we like it or not. They don't need our permission or our approval. So what happens when we say no to them? We suffer, plain and simple. Something beyond our control is happening, and we are mentally and energetically fighting it with our no. But when we fight what is, we actually give our power over to it.

When we take our attention away from the no and focus on the Yes!, we begin a 180-degree turn with our perception, and we take our power back in the process. Because behind every no-it-shouldn't-be-this-way is an invitation to say Yes!, to accept what is, and to face it with our Warrior Goddess spirit. When you shift your no to a Yes!, you are no longer a victim. Doing so is rarely easy, but you will see a radical shift in how you experience the world when you practice this.

Let's look at a couple examples of how this applies in real life.

Imagine you walk out your front door, late for work, when suddenly you step in a pile of dog poo. Can you see yourself saying no in this situation? How would you react? What happens in your body? You would probably tense up, recoil, and perhaps even curse out loud or even say something like, "Why me?" You might judge yourself for not paying attention to where you were walking, or get mad at your neighbor for not keeping their dog in their yard. If you maintain this state of mind, you will hold this clenched inner no as you scrub the poo from your shoe. And just like the unpleasant smell, your contraction lingers long after everything has been cleaned up.

Let's rewrite this story with the power of Yes! as your protagonist. Your shoe and the dog poo still connect, but this time you say, "Yes, that is dog poo!" The Yes! keeps you open and curious about what to do next. From a calm, this-is-what's-happening-let's-deal-with-it Warrior Goddess attitude, you clean your shoe. No drama, no blame, no upset. Clean up and move on. Perhaps you call your neighbor and ask them to keep their dog in their yard, and perhaps you call your office and tell them you'll be late. As you drive to work, you feel free and relaxed. You know that you will be arriving at the perfect time, whatever that turns out to be.

As you practice looking for the Yes! within every little situation like this one, you'll begin to rewire your being to live from Yes! to Yes!, like stepping-stones across the river. And then even in the super difficult situations you'll find the power of your Yes!

For instance, I recently heard about a Warrior Goddess woman who was diagnosed at the age of forty with breast cancer. On her first day of thirty-three days of radiation treatment she stood looking at her closet, trying to figure out what to wear. That's when she had an inspired idea, a way that could help her bring a Yes! to this difficult situation. She decided to wear a different dress for each day of her radiation. She dressed up in everything from old evening gowns she had tucked away at the back of her closet to new dresses she had bought just for the occasion, and even a couple dresses sent by friends and strangers. Rather than focusing on the "No, I don't want this to happen," she found a way to say "Yes! I am going to creatively celebrate each day of radiation." Doing this kept her inspired through the hard times and inspired many women around her as well.

One way to describe the big challenges that happen in our lives is as "plot twists." Your life is going down a certain comfortable story line, and then suddenly you encounter a "no, not this" moment: you or a loved one becomes chronically ill, you get laid off from your job of twenty years, or your house needs a new air conditioner in the middle of the hottest summer on record and you are struggling to pay for groceries.

This is where the Warrior Goddess path invites you to say Yes! Not "yes, I deserve this," or "yes, I agree with this," or even "yes, I like this." Rather, you say Yes! because it is happening, and doing so will help you show up fully and face this challenge with courage and grace, and you open yourself up to finding the unexpected or hidden gifts of the situation.

I want to be clear that saying Yes! does not mean we are passive and don't take action to try to change things when change is possible. We do not surrender to whatever is happening when we have other, better options. For many women I know, it's important to learn how to say a good, solid, from the belly "no." Many of us have been so conditioned to say yes when we want to say no, to give beyond our time and energy and resources, to wait until we are about to explode before making a boundary. These are not the situations I am speaking of, as learning to say no to others is actually saying yes to you.

Furthermore, saying Yes! doesn't mean we won't feel sadness or grief over the particular situation, and it certainly doesn't mean the road will suddenly become easy. But when you bring a Yes! to these situations rather than a no, you will find that this is where your true power lives.

A great way to begin practicing the art of saying Yes! is through internal and external cleaning. Because like it or not, life gets dirty. It gets messy. Even when we think we have cleared away the big traumas and messes of our past, thought patterns and feelings still come up from time to time, as do new situations that require our attention. This is the way of the world, and that's why implementing a regular cleaning and maintenance practice goes hand in hand with the practice of saying Yes! to life.

EIGHT

Yes! Cleaning
and Maintaining
the Home of You

Saying yes, opening up, and loving: these are
the keys that will unlock the prison door.
—Arnaud Desjardins

I magine living in a house that you never, ever cleaned. Visualize what it would look like if you never washed the dishes, never took out the garbage, never picked your clothes up off the floor, or vacuumed, or dusted—none of it. It wouldn't be long before you were wading knee high in stinky trash, searching through piles of smelly clothes to find something to wear, repulsed by icky food-encrusted dishes, and fighting off monster dust bunnies that had big, pointy teeth.

Now, imagine that you live in this home with your parents, siblings, childhood teachers, friends, anyone else who ever influenced you at a young age and all of their stuff, too. Finally, let's add in all your past partners and lovers as residents as well.

Not a pretty picture, is it?

While it's easy to visualize the chaos of a house not attended to, it's a bit more difficult to see the effects of not attending to one's inner home, or what I call the Home of You, but the results are the same: messy.

The Home of You is not the outer place where you sleep and eat, but the far more important home that is inside you. It is the home of your essence, your spark, your divine self. The Home of You is like a sacred temple that consists of four main areas: your mental being, your emotional being, your physical being, and your spiritual being. If we compare these inner elements to your outer home, we can say that your physical being is the structure of your house, your mental being is the electricity that powers it, your emotional being represents the ambience, and your spiritual being is that indescribable force of love that transforms a house into a home. These four elements are all woven together to form the one-of-a-kind, miraculous incarnation that is you.

Because you are here, reading this now, it means you have likely cleaned many parts of your inner home through the lessons of Warrior Goddess Training and the ones so far in the Warrior Goddess Way. But if you are like most women I know, your inner home is not an immaculate wonder of finalized organization and cleanliness, and it won't stay 100 percent junk-free without regular maintenance. Throughout any given day, emotional messes occur, feelings get spilled (or swept under the rug, ready to emerge again later), and thoughts of self-judgment or self-condemnation seem to come out of nowhere and clutter our headspace. This chapter is all about showing you how to create a regular maintenance plan to keep the Home of You clean and providing practice for saying Yes! to this cleaning process.

My use of your outer home as a metaphor for the Home of You is not by accident, as you can make a sacred connection between the care and maintenance of your inner being and the upkeep of your brick-and-mortar domicile. My friend and fellow author Stephanie Bennett Vogt has written extensively on this, beginning with her first book, *Your Spacious Self: Clear the Clutter and Discover Who You Are* (Hierophant 2012). As you will see in this chapter, what is good for the place you hang up your clothes can also be good for the place you hang your clothes on.

Maintenance as a Sacred Path: Merging the Inner and the Outer

Have you ever marveled at how fast nature can reclaim itself from civilization? Grass and weeds emerge from cracked sidewalks to soften edges and quickly begin the process of decomposing rock. Critters move into abandoned buildings and hasten their demise. Rain and sun steadily drain the color and strength of all they touch—even something as solid as an old pickup truck abandoned in a field.

Without constant care and awareness, entropy, or the tendency for nature to move from order to disorder in isolated systems, is the law. One moment you are happily wiping your hands after washing the dishes, and the next moment the sink is full again. You can straighten up a room in the morning so it is as neat as a soldier at attention and come back in the evening to find the space as disorderly as a drunken sailor.

If you are like me, you probably would prefer to clean something thoroughly one time and have it stay bright and shiny forever. But the reality is that all systems will tend toward disarray if left unattended. This includes everything from your laundry in the basket to the thoughts in your mind. From one day to the next, your life can shift from a sense of order to complete chaos. It's nothing personal; it's the way of the world, and just as you need to eat regularly and floors need to be swept often, your mind, emotions, and physical body all need consistent maintenance cleaning to stay at peace and healthy.

I invite you to experiment with linking the inner and the outer together, and rewire yourself to approach this maintenance with awareness and a sense of Yes! For instance, washing the dishes is the opportunity to come back to your breath and your stillness. Watering the plants is a way to commune with the plant world. Paying bills is a meditation on the ebb and flow of resources and a time to feel grateful for what you have. Cleaning the toilet and balancing your checkbook become part of your spiritual path rather than something to be done begrudgingly. Make home maintenance sacred and playful and see how much better you will feel about it. For most of us, tasks like these are concrete ways in which we can transform a no into Yes!

To maintain gracious inner sustenance, it is necessary to work at being present and aware of your thoughts, emotions, physical responses, and environment at all times. Your awareness will show you where you are getting lost in the messy areas of blaming, judging, or comparing (to name just a few dirty things). Keep your internal home clean by constantly *witnessing* your mind rather than *believing* your mind. Every time you notice heavy thoughts or emotions, put on your Warrior Goddess superhero of clean outfit and start scrubbing away the grime of nonacceptance and self-judgment that is muddying up your inner landscape.

Your witness is like a soapy sponge of love that washes the filthy particles of self-judgment. Through cleaning away the fear that is at the root of all messes, you can see your true reflection and act from your fullest integrity.

Internal maintenance does not necessarily involve getting rid of your thoughts or emotions, but it moves you toward no longer believing the mud-flinging voices in your head so you can tap into your unsoiled, pure, conscious self, and make choices from this clean, celebratory foundation.

Here are two real-life scenarios of linking external and internal cleaning. The first is a simple example of washing dishes; the second is about taking the actions of others personally.

Dirty Dishes

I used to be overrun by dirty dishes. Sometimes I was convinced that gremlins had come to my house the night before, had a party, and left their dishes for me to wash. I understood the need for maintenance, but many times I did not have the time or energy to wash after every meal. Because I really didn't like to wash dishes, after a few days my little kitchen sink looked more like a public hazard than a place to find clean water to drink or wash with.

After what seemed like decades of ineffectually trying to keep the dishes managed, I finally figured out the action necessary to make a system that worked for me, rather than my having to work for it. A few years ago I returned home from a vacation with renewed determination to change some old patterns. So I sat down to dream and implement a new dishwashing structure that moved me from frustrated to free.

The new structure I came up with was simple: I made an agreement with myself that I would wash the dishes each night before bed. What made this time different was my realization of how much it would shift my mornings if I woke up to a clean kitchen. I let myself off the hook of *trying* to wash dishes after every meal throughout the day and instead committed to washing the dishes each night *no matter what*, whether I was exhausted, or cranky, or it was late, or whatever other excuse my mind came up with. I kept this commitment because I knew the benefit of starting my morning off with a clean state of mind.

Then I added something that transformed my previously detested task into a sacred ritual with a clean focus: as I wash the dishes each night I also review my day, feeling gratitude for my experiences and friends, and releasing anything I do not need to take into my dreams down the drain with the sudsy rinse water. Like the kitchen sink, I wake up clear and ready for the day to come.

When I first started this new practice, there were days it felt hard, and my mind tried to be super helpful by coming up with plenty of excuses to not follow through on washing the dishes. But each night I keep choosing to say Yes! to myself, despite any resistance, and honor my commitment to go to bed only after the dishes were washed. I found that I went to bed each night feeling more free and clear, because I'd used that time to reflect on the day and release my own tension as I showed up with the water, the soap, and the dishes. And each morning my kitchen sparkled a cheery good morning to me. The physical spaciousness translated to more inner spaciousness, so my day started with a sense of possibility rather than the literal and emotional messiness of the past.

When you find a daily task that you are resistant to—flossing your teeth, driving to work, checking emails—this is a great place to practice bringing a conscious Yes! to your no. Watch how linking a new outer commitment to an inner sacred focus can not only help you keep the commitment but also transform your outlook and your experience in the process.

A Four-Step Process to Not Taking Things Personally

Anytime you take someone's words or actions personally, it's a cue that something from your inner world needs cleaning. When you take something personally, it is as if a spotlight is being turned toward a mess in a hidden corner of your being. You are not taking it personally because of someone else's mess, but because of how it is resonating with your own inner struggles.

Think about if you went to someone's house and their living room was dirty. You'd most likely notice the chaos, and you might or might not have some judgment about it. But you probably wouldn't believe that somehow you had caused the mess or that it was your fault it was there, even if they told you that you were to blame. You wouldn't take their mess or even the accusation that you caused it personally, because you would know it wasn't the truth.

While it's easy to see that you didn't mess up someone else's living room, that's often not the case when it comes to other, more complicated areas in our lives. Here's a real-life example of how a student of mine implemented a four-step process to help her stop taking someone's words and actions personally.

Gina arrived at one of our sessions highly frustrated, at the end of her proverbial rope over her stressful relationship with her mother. Despite having spent years cleaning up her past and practicing staying aware in the present during every phone call or visit to her mother, she would inevitably get triggered by something her mother would say or do, take her mother's words and actions personally, and then feel the familiar gunk of anger, sadness, and rebellion in the pit of her stomach. Sometimes the emotional hangovers of their encounters would be so great it would take days of spiritual practice before she reestablished a solid connection to her center again.

"I love my mother, and I'd really like to be able to spend time with her without feeling like I swallowed a giant tar ball," she told me.

Since I knew Gina had already done some major industrial-strength cleaning regarding her past relationship with her mom, which included forgiveness work as well as looking squarely at and taking responsibility for her own past actions with her mother, we now talked about a new method of cleaning to change their current and future interactions.

Here are the steps I gave Gina to help her clean up the current and future of her relationship with her mom. You can apply them to any relationship you have that is fraught with emotional muck.

1. Accept where you are. (Say Yes!)

2. Accept where the other person is. (Say Yes!)

3. Practice how you want to be in this situation.

4. Plan a different response for next time.

In this case, Gina took all four actions to heart. She shifted her perspective and stopped judging herself for still struggling with her relationship with her mom. She accepted her mother for exactly who she was, which included cleaning up any places within herself where she wanted her mother to be different. She noticed that she felt a similar reaction when she was around one of her coworkers, so she consciously spent more time around this person practicing acceptance and learning what exactly took her out of her center.

Then she made a list of all the ways she took her mother's words and actions personally and devised a new experiment: the next time she visited her mother she would do her best to listen to her and ask clarifying questions about what she was saying, instead of defending herself or arguing. She continually reminded herself that her mother's opinions were an expression of who her mother was only, and were not a factual account of Gina's experience or character. Finally, she made it a point to keep visits to two days or less, because she found that she could not hold her awareness and stay grounded for longer than this.

Over time, Gina's relationship with her mother changed completely. She still needed to be mindful of any accumulation of grit and grime in her being (which was usually caused by wanting her mother to be different), but now she experienced a sense of peace and gratitude when she visited her mother, where there once was only frustration and unhappiness.

When something is not working in your outer or inner home, do not blame yourself or others—but do not ignore the issue either. Turn and face the situation with a spirit of Yes! and a desire to identify the problem and clean it up. Be a blend of Nancy Drew and Heloise and rewire your mind to lovingly seek out good actions and solid systems that will clear any obstacles to cleanliness in your future. I have added some extra strength with cleaning bubbles exercises in the explorations section to help you practice this further. May your conscious cleaning bring more Yes! into the places of no and more ease into everything you do.

Yes!: Cleaning Resources

Gifts

- Reframing every no into an intentional Yes! is an act of self-love.

- When we say Yes! to the reality of daily maintenance, we create more ease and flow in every day.

- Taking things personally points to hidden messes that are now spotlighted by our emotional reaction. Say Yes! and explore what is ready to be cleaned within.

Explorations

CLEANING THE OUTER AND THE INNER

In this exercise, we will look at a three-step process to help you clean the inner and the outer. A note of practicality: I am grouping the inner and outer cleanings together here to make a sacred connection, but at first you may find it better to do steps 1, 2, and 3 for your outer home and then go back and do them for your inner home.

Step 1: Notice What Needs to Be Cleaned Without Tracking in More Mud

You wouldn't put on filthy work boots and stomp through your house to figure out what room in your home you wanted to clean first. Similarly, be careful not to bring a judgmental attitude into your inner home to help you assess what needs your immediate attention. Remember, the first step is always to notice, or witness, what needs cleaning. It only makes it worse when we further judge our surroundings or ourselves for needing another cleaning. Everyone and everything needs regular cleaning, and bringing your judge into the process is similar to smearing dog poo on your carpets and wondering why they continue to smell. Bring the spirit of the nonjudgmental witness as you do the following work.

For your outer home, take off your shoes and do a room-to-room tour as if you were visiting for the first time (and yes, this includes your closets!). Resist the temptation to muddy things up by comparing, wishing, or griping about anything you see here. Simply notice what you find in your exterior world, and ask yourself the following questions: What would you likely change in the room if you were seeing it for the first time? What items do not feed your soul or make you smile when you look at them? What additions would make it feel homier? Is there anything present that you have been meaning to clean, fix, or remove but haven't done yet? Don't take action right now; just notice. I recommend grabbing a notepad and making notes as you move from room to room. If the idea of going to more than one room overwhelms you, just do this for one room for right now.

For your inner home, take a moment to review your mental, emotional, physical, and spiritual state. Once again, be sure to set aside your inner judge and simply survey the inner landscape from a witness point of view. How are you feeling physically today? How is your mental attitude? What's happening with your emotions? What types of thoughts have you experienced? What stories has your mind been spinning? Are you feeling connected to your spirit? Are you feeling grounded in the present moment? Regretful of the past? Worried about the future? Be curious and simply notice anything that is causing you pain, suffering, or discomfort today and see if you can find the source. Like you did with your outer home, jot down some notes about what you witnessed.

Step 2: Note What Needs to Be Cleaned or Removed

Now that you have assessed what's happening on the outside and inside, it's time to decide what needs to be cleaned or changed. You create space in your inner and outer world by either jettisoning or otherwise resolving any mental or physical issue that weighs you down. In this step, you are going to write down the action step you could take in order to clean up any issue you identified in step 1.

For your outer home, look at the items around your house. What items don't spark your soul or serve a useful purpose? If you don't use something and you don't love it, what is it doing here? In other words, ask yourself, "Do I really need this? How is it benefiting me?" If you are really nervous about whether it is time to let something go or not, put it in a box and hold on to it for a while to see if you ever think about it again. And remember, if you once loved some things and now don't, or if you never loved them, someone else probably will. Pass these items on to someone who might love or use them. Take them to a thrift store, give them to friends, or take them to work and see if they spark anyone.

Next, is there any cleaning or other project you've been meaning to get to but haven't yet? Have you swept things under the rug or in the closet? Is there something that needs repair? Finally, would rearranging your current items change the energy in your home? Be open to any new possibilities that arise to you in the moment, and write these action steps in your notepad.

For your inner home, how are you feeling physically, mentally, emotionally, and spiritually? What areas need to be cleaned, and how could you do so? For instance, when our bodies get hungry, tired, or ill, that can affect our mood. Is it time for a meal or a nap? And if you find yourself in a situation where a nap or a meal isn't an option, can you instead be aware that your mood may be "off" because your physical needs aren't being met? Proceed with caution in these circumstances.

If you notice that your thoughts or emotions are off balance, oftentimes just talking to a grounded voice (a member of your sangha) can help you find your center. I have a dear friend who says, "the secret is in the sharing," and what he means is that just by talking about what's troubling us, we often feel better—even if the situation itself doesn't change.

Finally, what action steps could you take if you are feeling spiritually off balance? Perhaps one of the meditations found earlier in this book is in order or saying a silent prayer or repeating a mantra. Remember, just write down the possible action steps. We will look at doing them in the next step.

Step 3: Time for Action, One Step at a Time

Many times we want to clean up the environment of our inner and outer worlds, but if we focus on everything that needs to be done all at once, it's easy to become overwhelmed and give up altogether. A simple trick is to concentrate solely on one area to clean at a time. Keep your attention narrow rather than broad, so you feel confident in your capacity to create transformation.

For your outer home, start with the room where you spend the most time and choose one thing from your list to clean, fix, or rearrange. Focus completely on this task and do nothing else until it's finished. After it's complete, check it off your list and then decide if you have the time and energy to go on to another item or it's better to put the list away for the day. Be careful to not beat yourself up here for not doing enough, and instead choose to celebrate the success.

For your inner home, ask yourself, When you did your internal surveying, what is the place that needs the most attention? Was it your mental, emotional, spiritual, or physical self that you need to focus on right now? Once you have identified the area that needs your immediate attention, focus only on cleaning that area. What action step can you take to do so (share your feelings with a friend, get something to eat, meditate)? Do this one thing first, check it off your list, and proceed to the next item if time and energy allow.

MAKING CLEANING TASKS MANAGEABLE

Like we covered in the previous exercise, one of the keys to implementing a regular maintenance plan that works is to keep your tasks manageable. For this exercise, I want you to pick one area in either your outer home or your inner home to address. Next, ask yourself, "Does this task feel doable?" If the answer is no, then the next step is to cut the proposed action into bite-size pieces in order to make it more manageable. Below are two examples of what I mean.

- At home: Clean your garage.

- Reality: Depending on what your garage looks like, this task could be way too big and vague. Break it down. Focus on the first itty-bitty baby step, and give yourself a time frame. Your bigger goal is to clean the garage, but break it up into nuggets of actionable ease.

- Itty-bitty doable step: Gather all tools into one area by Wednesday. Celebrate by letting yourself feel the awesomeness of knowing where to go to find the screwdriver you want. Nice. Pick your next itty-bitty step for cleaning the garage.

As a side note, some of you may find it helpful to discover when your optimal cleaning time is, depending on when your energy is the highest for these tasks. This might be 6:00 a.m., noon, or midnight, depending on your own personal makeup. If you have an optimal cleaning time, make an agreement with yourself to keep that time open for these types of tasks. Create a supportive atmosphere by putting on your favorite music or otherwise pampering yourself.

- At home: Clear out the fear of strangers that I inherited from my mother.

- Reality: Again, this task is way too big and vague. Bring it into the first itty-bitty baby step, and give yourself a time frame.

- Itty-bitty doable step: On my way home from work each day, I spend five minutes sitting in my favorite park as I practice relaxing and breathing deeply while watching strangers. (Once you complete the task, don't forget to congratulate yourself for your courage and stick-to-itiveness. Then pick your next itty-bitty step for clearing your fear of strangers.

The point of this exercise is this: anytime you feel overwhelmed by an inner or outer cleaning project, the solution is to break it down into smaller (sometimes super tiny) action steps.

CLEANING GOSSIP

Your words (both the ones you say only to yourself and the ones you speak aloud) are immensely powerful. Bring your attention to cleaning your communication, both the verbal and the nonverbal, with yourself and those in your life.

One good place to focus on is gossip. Gossip can arise in very, very subtle forms. Bring your cleaning awareness to where you participate in gossip, and how gossip creates messes both with the people you gossip to and within yourself.

Take a week to consciously refrain from any gossip. If you do find yourself gossiping, simply witness the results and how you feel. Watch how rapidly gossip can spread and affect others, like tar balls on the beach that get tracked everywhere.

SEPARATING MAINTENANCE FROM PROJECTS

A project has a start and an end and anywhere from one to hundreds of steps in between.

Maintenance is an ongoing process, without no end point. If you want to live in a nice house or drive a car that's reliable, it is necessary to engage in this work.

To distinguish maintenance from projects, make two lists: one of your home projects and one of maintenance actions. "Clean the garage" is a project, whereas "keep the garage clean" is maintenance. "Go to the dentist" is a project (find the phone number, set up an appointment, show up for the appointment, get gifted a new toothbrush), whereas "floss my teeth daily" is maintenance.

Now, for every maintenance action on your list, write down approximately how long it would require and how often you would like to do it. Just an estimate is fine. If you do not know, guess and then keep track of how much time it actually takes or what amount of time you can give that particular maintenance task.

For example, "Keep the garage clean" is fleshed out with "Keep the garage clean for fifteen minutes, once a week."

"Washing dishes" is completed by, "Washing dishes for ten minutes, after meals or before I go to bed every night."

This list will help you schedule regular maintenance, so you do not end up with more projects. (Choosing not to take regular action for garage maintenance eventually turns into the daunting "clean the garage" project.)

NINE

Yes! Relationships

It only takes one person to change your life: you.
—Ruth Casey

I magine waking up every day, putting your hand on your heart, and saying to yourself, "Good morning, beloved. We are going to have an amazing day today!" Imagine that each evening you give yourself a hug, say, "I love you so much— thank you for being you!" and review everything you are grateful for about yourself before falling asleep. Imagine that every time you looked at yourself in the mirror you were delighted by what you saw, and anytime you were having a really difficult day at work, or you were not feeling well physically, you quietly whispered to yourself, "I'm here for you, and we will get through today one step at a time." What if you could be such a cheerleader, best friend, and creative vixen of love for yourself that every day was a celebration no matter what life presented?

Now *that* would be a fulfilling relationship, wouldn't it?

As we begin this chapter on Warrior Goddess relationships, let's put aside figuring out how to find the right partner or trying improve your relationship with your current partner, or your parents, or your children, or whomever. First and foremost, this is about saying Yes! to you, so let's go inside first and ask yourself the following question: What can you do to fall deeply, thoroughly, and endlessly in love with yourself?

Believe it or not, doing so is the secret to the art of all good relationships, because all your relationships have one person in common: you. When you engage with others from a place of self-love, your relationships improve exponentially, because you are no longer dependent on the other for your happiness.

The irony is that one of the keys to loving yourself can be found in learning how to genuinely receive from others and the world. This may sounds counterintuitive, but it's true. Allow me to explain why I feel that, as women, the first step to developing a healthy relationship with ourselves is to put receiving before giving.

The Art of Receiving

So many women I know are exhausted and functioning near empty, giving our best from low reserves. I see it all the time, and I have experienced it myself. This inner depletion stems from the belief that we have to put everyone else first, that we must strive for nothing short of perfection, and that we must be liked for our service or acknowledged for our work. But ultimately living your life this way will leave you feeling run-down and exhausted—mentally, physically, emotionally, and spiritually depleted.

What I have found is that the more exhausted, overworked, or otherwise depleted you feel, the more you need to learn to receive. The busier you are, the more you need to slow down. When you feel there is no time for anything else in your life, that's proof that you definitely need to make space to be welcoming. The irony is that it's actually when you learn to receive that you become full, and the type of receiving I am speaking of is the art of saying Yes! to everything that shows up to support you in the present moment.

Imagine if you had dropped a copper penny into a piggy bank on every hour of each day you were alive. At the age of fifty you would have saved $4,380.

If you saved a dime for every hour, that would be $43,800.

If you saved a dollar for every hour, that would be $438,000.

Every hour of every day, learning how to slow down and receive and accept the support that is around you is actually what can fill your inner bank account. Start with a penny-sized action. Pause and take one breath and look up at the beauty of the sky as it brings rain or sunshine, both of which are vital to your long-term sustenance. Place one hand on your heart and one hand on your belly and say thank you to the center of your being, as it shows up again and again to support you throughout the day. Take a moment to stretch toward the sky and then bend down to touch your toes, noticing how every square inch of your body is exactly where it needs to be at this moment and serves as your constant support.

Then build your receiving capacity to a dime-sized action every hour. Spend five minutes walking in nature, taking in the colors of the beautiful art show. Close your eyes and imagine breathing in peace for a few moments, then take a break from your work and do one yoga pose with a smile. The world is trying to support you in so many ways, but so many of us don't notice this. Learning how to recognize and accept the support that is all around you is the art of receiving in action.

And in those all-important moments when other humans are directly giving gifts to you, recognize and be grateful for these gems instead of minimizing them. For example, when someone tells you "thank you," take a moment to stop, look him or her in the eye, take that love in, and say, "you are welcome." This is true human-to-human receiving.

When a stray cat comes and twines around your ankles, stop, stroke, and take in the abundant love of that purr. (As I wrote this, while sitting at an outside table of a hotel in Mexico, a black-and-white cat came out of nowhere and jumped onto my lap. Purring commenced. I stopped to take in the kitty love. Cats are the best reminders of how to blissfully receive.) Each time you drink a glass of water or eat a meal, take in the earth gifting you blessings of life. Notice the sunsets and the smell of baking bread, the smile of a stranger and the beauty of your grandmother's wrinkled hand.

There is so much to receive. So much is freely given, every second, for you to be filled by, drop by drop. And it's all trying to support you, if you will only stop to notice it. You deserve all these gifts. In fact, it is your birthright to collect them and become so filled with the holy mundane moments that all you can do is start to overflow.

As you practice in a thousand tiny penny ways, your ability to receive will grow naturally. Instead of rushing to the next thing on your list, you will take five minutes to quietly sit and enjoy the wind. And in this way, you develop a relationship with yourself where you become your own best friend and lover, because through the art of receiving you learn how to respect and honor your own needs.

Then, rather than saying yes to someone else's request without thought, you will feel into your needs and perhaps say yes to yourself and a "no, thank you," to them by choosing to take a break, or do what really nourishes you instead. Rather than dodging a compliment or diminishing someone's praise of your accomplishments, you will get soft, let the moment penetrate your heart, and respond with a "yes, thank you."

When we learn to receive, we get full on the inside by reconnecting with the love that is always radiating from the trees and from the eyes of children. Then we stop trying to fill the hole in our hearts with another thing we don't need, like a new purse, or new shoes, or a new relationship, and instead become full of gratitude for the myriad things that show up to help us in every moment. And in those moments when the going gets really difficult, we naturally remind ourselves that this too shall pass, and know that our deepest, most profound work in the moment is to keep receiving even as we give.

When we get good at receiving from the world, we naturally start to send and receive love to ourselves. Then, when you wake in the morning, you can say to yourself, "good morning, beautiful. I love you, and I am going to support you unconditionally today." This is saying Yes! to yourself, always and in all ways.

From this important relationship work of receiving and crafting a new relationship with yourself, you can then expand this solid core of self-love and acceptance to your outer relationships. As you will see in the next section, all of your relationships, from the difficult to the sublime, are a perfect mirror back to your relationship with yourself.

The Reflection of Relationships

As you have likely noticed, it's our connection or disconnection to friends, family, beloveds, coworkers, neighbors, children, strangers, and especially ourselves that makes our hearts sing or sink. That's the way it is for most of us humans. When we are in love, everything is sunrises and stars and song. There is nothing that we cannot do or be. Everyone is beautiful, and all problems overcomeable.

A dear friend of mine witnessed an encounter that demonstrates the mirror effect of relationships quite perfectly. She was having lunch with two newly connected lovers when, a few minutes into the meal, one lover's fork slipped, and his paper plate catapulted across the table. His lunch landed squarely on his beloved's chest, splattering lettuce and oily salad dressing all over her new silk shirt. As he awkwardly attempted to wipe the mess off, he only managed to smear it further, yet his beloved turned to my friend with a smile and a sweet sigh and said, "Oh, isn't he wonderful?"

Most of us have had this type of experience at some point in our lives, when we can only see love when we look at another (we all did as babies, looking into our parents' or caretakers' eyes for the first time). Wouldn't it be wonderful if this initial bliss stayed with us forever? But the truth is, when you lose touch with these feelings of love, any relationship can quickly get messy. Imagine the same lunch spill scenario happening between a couple that was struggling over financial issues, or between competitive sisters, or between coworkers who were having trouble finishing an overdue report.

Even when we really want to constantly love (or at least be nice to) others, we all know that it's not that easy sometimes. But the truth is that all relationships are a perfect reflection of your relationship with yourself. And yes, I mean all of them, all the time. Consequently, every time you judge another; every angry or jealous or competitive reaction; every instance when you caretake or feel sorry for someone; every time you mentally, emotionally, or physically abuse another;

every experience that you take personally; and every time you close your heart to another, you are doing this to yourself also.

And every place where you take others' abuse or neglect or lack of love and use it against yourself is a mirror of where you are abusing, neglecting, or not loving yourself.

Let's talk more about this, as it can be a difficult concept to grasp.

All of our relationships show us a clear reflection of our own beliefs about ourselves. When we stop pointing figures (blame) or shift from feeling helplessly broken (shame and victimhood), we can look into the reflection before us with curiosity. And what the reflection shows us is our own feelings of lack or abundance of self-love.

Mirror, Mirror

In every interaction with someone else there are always two reflections: the mirror of what is actually happening and the reflection that is created by our reaction to what is happening.

The mirror of what is actually happening is the facts. A mirror reflects reality without trying to understand, fix, judge, or justify it. A mirror simply shows what is happening in front of us.

The second mirror comes from the reflection of our own beliefs and stories. While we cannot always choose or change what is happening in the first mirror of reality, we can change how we are perceiving the world.

To do this, you shift your focus from what is happening on the outside, and instead look at how you are inwardly responding to what is happening.

What is being reflected is your inner story playing out in front of you. And your true power comes when you have the courage to say Yes! and turn to face this inner mirror. Get quiet. Breathe. Be curious. What do you see reflected in the space between another's action and your reaction?

When your insides are upset about something that's happening on the outside, look within and ask yourself: What is there for me to see in this situation? What is there for me to learn about myself? What or whom am I trying to control, and why? What am I afraid of? By exploring these questions you can use the reflection in a way that will bring you freedom instead of chaining you to endless cycling of an old story.

Let's explore this inner mirror right now by imagining the following scenarios.

What reflection do you see when someone you care about

• Withdraws their love and attention?

• Is angry with you?

• Says something that hurts your feelings?

• Doesn't do what you wish they would do?

What is your response to these types of experiences? Do you withdraw your own love and attention? Do you get angry with yourself or them? Do you abandon yourself? Do you argue against reality, and in so doing take your attention away from loving yourself? Do you judge and berate them in your mind?

Awareness of what's happening inside you is the first step to transforming an inner no into a Yes! in these situations. It's the beginning of cleaning our old, false beliefs so we can see everything with the sparkle of our own self-love.

Cleaning Our Distorted Reflections

When we first fall in love or make a new close friend, we feel full. We experience a sense of being seen, being understood, being cherished. What we are feeling is real, a reflection of our capacity to love and be loved. It feels divine.

And that's the easy part. What we are experiencing is "I love that this person loves me. I love that this person sees me. I love that this person understands me." But what is really happening is we are tapping into our own natural state of unconditional love. Someone else might be stimulating that sense of love, but we are the ones experiencing it, and therefore we are the ones creating it—which means it is our love we are feeling.

So the salad dressing all over our silk blouse is fantastic, because we are experiencing unconditional love. We love the other person's faults, glitches, and unskillful eating disasters. I believe these times are precious, because they give us a sense of the depth of love that we have inside of us. But they are temporary, because we have not yet understood that this love is a reflection of our own love.

And so it can get really confusing when suddenly the reflections we see with a beloved or dear friend shift. They are being themselves: sometimes dorky, sometimes inconsiderate, sometimes insensitive. And where we once radiated love, we start to be eaten by irritation, anger, or hopelessness.

This is where real work comes in.

Here is an example. Sally was visiting her friend Laura, whom she was really excited to see. But at the same time Sally was visiting, another friend of Laura's, Brigit, was also staying at her house.

On Sally's second day there, Brigit and Laura had a meeting to go to, so Sally happily stayed at Laura's house and caught up on her emails. That is, she was happy until she realized Brigit and Laura had been gone for three and a half hours. At first Sally felt worried, then abandoned. Her mind started making up all sorts of stories: "Sally likes Brigit more than me. She doesn't want to be my friend but she doesn't know how to tell me. She wishes I wasn't at her house. She only wants to spend time with Brigit, but she feels obligated since I'm here. Maybe I should leave. I should just pack my bags and go home since Sally doesn't want me here."

Luckily, Sally had enough awareness to realize that the situation was reflecting something really important within her. She brought her attention away from Laura and Brigit and back to the mirror that was being shown to her. And what she saw in the reflection was a lot of assumptions and internal fears.

She also saw that the place to focus was not on Laura's behavior or her fears that Laura didn't care about her. The important reflection was that Sally was taking the assumptions offered by her mind about the situation and then using those assumptions against herself. She saw that these assumptions were the product of her fears, which were rooted in her history of not loving and being there for herself, of abandoning herself, and of a deep-seated fear of not feeling worthy.

By seeing the reflection of her own inner judgment and fears, Sally was able to bring more loving compassion to herself and realize all of this was going on inside her, not in the world. (She actually had no idea where Laura and Brigit were, since she hadn't spoken with them since they left.) So when Laura and Brigit came home, she could greet them with an open heart and laugh with them about their story of two women in skirts and heels trying to fix the flat tire on Brigit's car.

The -isms and You

One more important note here for women (especially women of color, gay women, transgender women, or otherwise marginalized women). You will see and experience sexism, racism, classism, homophobia, and fear all around you, as it is unfortunately insidious, like a toxic weed. What is important is to notice where you subtly believe these lies and anyplace you are diminishing, demeaning, or denying yourself.

You can use any experiences of this type of rejection and fear to bring awareness to your own inner landscape and to love yourself even more fiercely. Patiently weed out any self-rejection to fully own your magnificence, regardless of anyone else's projection.

Throughout all the Warrior Goddess books we've discussed the importance of unconditional self-love and self-acceptance, and as you practice this and develop this toward yourself, you'll notice how you more easily and readily extend this to others as well. This doesn't mean that you accept inappropriate or harmful behavior that others try to inflict upon you, as in fact it's your own self-love that now powers you to say Yes! to yourself and no to others when they act toward you in ways that don't respect your true worth. But instead of trying to control others, or change them, or wish they were different, you can now see them with eyes of compassion (and this includes compassionately calling the authorities if you are in an abusive situation). You know that their inappropriate behavior is a reflection of their own self-judgment and self-rejection, and you know this because you recognize that you once did that to yourself.

When we see a relationship through the eyes of attachment, fear, a need to control, or fantasy, then we aren't seeing through the eyes of authentic love. These items stem from a sense of lack. Authentic love flows from a deep well of abundance, a fullness of being that cannot help but spill over and nourish others. This kind of love is like the proverbial loaves and fishes because everyone gets fed.

May we all hold our hands out to each other to lift each other up when we forget, or get scared, or feel beaten down by the force of another's unconsciousness. And may we all continue to educate, speak out, take a stand, and creatively transform ignorance, intolerance, and prejudice, starting with the radical act of saying Yes! to our unique, authentic, wise, and wonderful selves. In this way, we let the Yes! of love radiate outward to others regardless of their misconceptions. You become a radical Yes! bomb of love toward your beloved, your family, and strangers when your attention stays on yourself rather than trying to change others.

The Power of Intent

When difficulties arise in any relationship, another tool is to ask yourself, "What is my intent in this relationship now?" Note that I did not say ask yourself what you did wrong, or what the other person did wrong, as these types of questions just set us up for blame and judgment. There is a time and place for that type of inventory, but to use the tool of intent let's stay focused on this one simple question.

Your intent is your focus. And once you know what your intent is, you can use it to bring more awareness of your inner patterns into the open, choose the best course of action, and help heal any of your old wounding in the process. Below is an example from my own life to further explain this.

One of my most painful relationship experiences came at the end of my first marriage. The truth was that it was time for our relationship to shift, but I stubbornly held on. My intent at the time was: "I will stay and keep working on this relationship no matter what. I will fight for it. I will not abandon it." I refused to see what was in front of me.

At some point I decided, "He will have to leave. I am not going to end our marriage," and so I stayed long after my husband's heart had left the relationship. I dug my heels in. I kept hoping something would shift. In hindsight, I can see that my intent was strong, but it was misdirected. I was using my energy to try to control him and the situation, trying to force something that clearly wasn't working for either of us anymore.

Fast-forward three years to a new relationship. I shared a bit about my experience in an earlier chapter, and here is how my intent helped me stay true and say Yes! to myself. On my fourth visit with my new romantic interest, I made an agreement with myself: to show up and really see what was there. I committed to bringing my full heart forward, to honestly exploring if it was a good match, and to see if I would be met fully.

At the end of the visit I had learned a few things: I really, really liked this man. A lot. I felt we were a beautiful match intellectually, spiritually, sexually, and socially. (Oh, the sex!) I realized I had healed from the heartbreak of the end of my marriage and I was ready to say Yes! and to step into intimate relationship again. Yay!

And I also realized that he was not showing up in the way I deeply desired.

Damn.

I found myself looking into the mirror of this relationship and not wanting to see the truth, and I noticed how my mind quickly started to make up stories: If I just stuck it out then he would want to be with me; I just needed to be patient, and I should settle for what he could give me because we are such a good match.

I also saw that he was mirroring to me the ways I had not shown up in my relationships fully in the past. I saw myself reflected in his actions: how I would often stay busy to avoid intimacy, how I had not allowed myself to be vulnerable, how I had been emotionally unavailable to my past beloveds. It was hard medicine to be on the receiving end of what I recognized as my own familiar behaviors. And the healing for me was in forgiving myself for where I hadn't show up in the past, being mature enough to not try to change someone else, and in acknowledging my own growth in relationships. Yes!

When I brought my Yes! to the present moment and really stopped and looked at the reality of the situation, it was obvious that we were in different places and wanted different things. When I got quiet I could feel in my soul the truth: I was ready to be emotionally met and show up fully in a relationship. And he was not. Period. End of story. I could make up all sorts of reasons why, tell myself if I just stuck with it long enough it would change (hmm, that sounds familiar, eh?). But I went inside and asked myself, *What is your intent in this relationship?* And the answer was, *To love this human exactly where he is, and to love myself exactly where I am.*

And so I applied more soapy love, and I let the dream of a romantic partnership go so I could show up fully for myself and for our friendship.

In doing so I honored myself, I honored all the gifts of this human who had helped me heal so much, and I could then show up for a friendship with this amazing being without demanding or endlessly longing for him to be any different.

And there are times I still wish things were different, I still hope it might change, and I still wonder if I could have done anything differently. But I quickly bring myself back to my intent: to love the truth. To love this human exactly where he is, and to love myself exactly where I am, period.

Naming my Yes! then also allowed me to clarify what I was desiring in a relationship and, instead of putting that all on one person, to open to how I could find my craving in my other close relationships and with myself. My Yes! has led to more intimate friendships, more quiet time with myself, and a sense of healing by owning and forgiving myself for my past behaviors.

When we are clear on our intent in each of our relationships, we give ourselves a guiding star to turn toward as we navigate the sometimes choppy waters and scary depths of intimacy and connection. But we must make sure that our intent is not about changing the other person, and that we are not using our words and energy to judge or blame ourselves or another.

My prayer for all of us Warrior Goddesses is that we use *every* relationship in our life, from the easy to the challenging, as a way to soften our hard, brittle edges and to strengthen our power to take new actions from an inner Yes! guided by our intent.

In closing this chapter, I'd like to share with you the following fabulous fable, written by an unknown author and popularly referred to as the parable of the three hairs.

A woman woke up one morning and noticed she had only three hairs on her head. "*Hmmmm*," she said, "I think I'll braid my hair today." She did, and she had a great day.

The next morning she woke up and saw that only two hairs remained on her head. "Well," she said, "I'm going to part my hair today." She did, and she had a really fun day.

The following morning she awoke to only one hair on her head. "Oh," she said, "I think I'll wear my hair in a ponytail today." She did, and her day was wonderful.

The next morning she awoke to find that she did not have a single hair on her head. "Yay!" she said. "I don't have to fix my hair today!"

I love this story because it exemplifies the power of two things: saying Yes! to what is, and the power of being in a loving relationship with yourself, no matter what. This is the type of Warrior Goddess relationship I want for you, to love and support yourself no matter what. You deserve nothing less.

Yes!: Relationship Resources

Gifts

- ◆ When we take responsibility for learning how to receive, we have much more to give.

- ◆ "What is my intent in this relationship now?" is a vital question to create a new north star for our focus and actions.

- ◆ Trying to change others takes us away from the one place we can make change: within.

Explorations

RIDING THE WILD PONY OF RELATIONSHIPS

I was blessed as a young woman to have many passionate relationships with horses. They taught me lessons about myself and relationships, and what I learned was that in many ways relationships are often like the unpredictable and slightly wild racetrack thoroughbreds I rode as a teenager. Following are five tips on how to ride the wild pony of relationships, plus a divination practice for when you're feeling stuck or confused about what to do next in a specific relationship.

Approach with Presence and Patience

Horses are incredibly sensitive to the energetic state of humans. And humans are, too. If you approach a horse with a sense of fear, self-doubt, or contraction, they will be hesitant and standoffish with you. Approach a horse with patience, presence, and openness, and even the most skittish one will come over to check you out and say hello. The same is true with your relationships, so be sure to approach them with curiosity rather than demand.

Ride from Your Center

One thing you learn in the saddle right away is don't try to be fancy; sit deep and stay present. Leaning too far in one direction or another, trying to help or fix others, will cause you to end up in a pile on the ground. Relationships also have their ups and downs, so when you feel the pull of drama, anger, or blame, remember to return to your heart center. This is the art of staying grounded when something unexpected happens to knock you off balance.

Don't Jerk on the Reins

If you pull the reins too hard, or back and forth, then your horse gets confused and doesn't know what you want. Tugging on the reins only creates more resistance and struggle.

Similarly, it's important to communicate your feelings, wants, and needs clearly to the other in your relationship as well. When you speak your truth from your heart, you are doing your part to maintain clear communication.

Look Where You're Going

When you're riding, you learn to let your eyes and focus guide the direction of the horse. You don't look back, because you're not headed that direction. In relationships, it's good to learn from the past, but you don't want to keep your focus there. Keep your eyes forward if you want to move forward. A soft, focused gaze allows your peripheral vision to note potential obstacles and for you to make adjustments. What is your intent for this relationship now? Where do you want it to go in the future?

Dismount Gracefully

Sometimes a horse and a rider just aren't a good match, either for a day or even a lifetime. If, despite following the above steps, your relationship ride is not working, it might be time to stop and step down. Sometimes the best gift you can give a relationship is to take some space (an hour, a day, or a week) to get centered again in your heart and with your intent. And sometimes this means consciously ending a relationship. We can bring grace to the dismount by holding as much compassion and gratitude as possible for the gifts and learnings of a relationship as we consciously bring it to a close.

Going Deeper

The following divination practice is for when you're feeling stuck or confused about what to do next in a specific relationship.

On five different pieces of paper or index cards, write down the five tips from this chapter for riding the wild pony of relationship:

- Approach with presence and patience

- Ride from your center

- Don't jerk on the reins

- Look where you're going

- Dismount gracefully

Turn the pieces of paper or index cards facedown on a table, and mix them up. Think of the relationship that you're seeking some guidance on. Hold the name of the person in your mind and pick up one of the cards. What is your message or lesson?

TEN

Yes! Opening to the Endings

Life will break you. Nobody can protect you from that, and living alone won't either, for solitude will also break you with its yearning. You have to love. You have to feel. It is the reason you are here on earth. You are here to risk your heart. You are here to be swallowed up. And when it happens that you are broken, or betrayed, or left, or hurt, or death brushes near, let yourself sit by an apple tree and listen to the apples falling all around you in heaps, wasting their sweetness. Tell yourself you tasted as many as you could.

—Louise Erdrich

When we say Yes! to any relationship, we are also opening ourselves to vulnerability and loss. Beginnings become endings become beginnings again. There is no avoiding this. Every bite of food you eat that keeps you alive is a result of the end of a life, plant or animal. Every day we lose people, pets, and our youth. Even the most permanent of relationships—parents, spouses, children, self—will end in someone's death. Always. No exceptions.

I'm not trying to be morose here, but as we move into the final lesson of the Warrior Goddess Way, I want to bring our attention back to the incredible gift life is, how precious it is, and how fleeting. And also how incredibly brave we need to be to embrace it fully, passionately, and completely, which is the Warrior Goddess Way.

We can try to manage life, limit our loving, create barriers against loss. But all we are doing is numbing ourselves and missing the exquisiteness of being fully alive—because life is death, and death is life. They are the same. When we try to pretend that death doesn't exist, that it won't come for us and everyone we know, we have our heads buried in the sand of avoidance. When we welcome both life and death, we can bring our wonder and gratitude to the ebb and the flow. Our grief at someone's passing then becomes a holy, sacred garden filled with the scents and colors of those we shared it with.

The Toltecs have a beautiful goddess of death that we call the Angel of Death. The Angel is not some scary grim reaper figure, but a compassionate, loving being who walks with us all the time. She loans us our life and everything in it, from our children to our car to our physical body, and at any moment she can come and reclaim what is hers. We learn to not be afraid of her, but to see her as a true ally and friend. She reminds us to stay present, to show up fully, to not be complacent.

I still struggle with endings; they are never easy. But I have learned to stay open, honor my emotions (especially the love), and let go to the mystery of death. I consider the Angel of Death my best friend and sacred companion. Let me explain how this came about.

Befriending Death

I learned about the Angel of Death from my longtime mentor and friend, don Miguel Ruiz, author of *The Four Agreements* and likely the most well-known Toltec teacher on the planet. At the end of February in 2002, he gave me a great gift.

He died.

Well, he almost died.

In the middle of the night, don Miguel woke up in the midst of a massive heart attack. Being a medical doctor, he understood the severity of his heart's struggle. Later, at the hospital, he called together his sons to tell them he was going to die and to say good-bye. I received a phone call later that day. Miguel was still alive but was not expected to live long. He had slipped into a coma after losing most of his heart's function.

When I got off the phone, I sat on a creaky wooden swing next to a massive banyan tree. I was in Maui, Hawaii, with a group of people, most of whom knew don Miguel. It was 7:00 a.m. The birds were flitting and singing, the grass was growing undisturbed, and the sky was shaking off her golden dawn robe to uncover her light blue morning gown.

As I rocked myself on the swing and thought about my first journey to Maui with don Miguel many years earlier, I was surprised to notice that I felt no sadness, only an immense gratitude. I would dearly miss my beloved teacher's open smile, his coyote wisdom, and the full-being heart hugs that he unself-consciously gave to everyone he met. And my being was filled with two realizations: First, without a doubt, I knew that Miguel loved me. And second, without a doubt, Miguel knew that I loved him.

There was nothing more I needed to say or do. Our relationship was complete, nothing was unspoken or in need of clearing. I could feel him in my bones, and I knew that no matter where his spirit traveled, a little bit of me was within him as well. I understood at depth that death was not an ending, just a slight broadening of the space between us.

Miguel remained in a coma for almost three months. For two months I could feel his presence, even stronger than I had when he was in good health. And then one afternoon during the third month of his coma, he suddenly disappeared energetically. It was as if his spirit had been hanging around me, continuing to teach and guide me, and then one day he was called away on other duties.

When I called my Toltec community peers, many had had the same experience. The physical being of Miguel was still alive, hooked to many machines in a hospital in Los Angeles. But his spirit had traveled beyond reach. The void left behind was palpable and strange, similar to when I shaved my head after having long hair most of my life. And, while I missed being able to feel him, I still knew two things to be true: I knew that Miguel loved me, and Miguel knew that I loved him. My heart was full, even if I missed the subtle weight of his presence.

One morning, Miguel's shape seemed to materialize behind a friend I was talking to. I jumped up and said, "Miguel is back!" A quick phone call confirmed that, indeed, Miguel had woken up from his coma and was back in the realm of the living.

Five years after Miguel woke up from his coma, my father's death brought another gift and another lesson. My father passing after years of actively fighting leukemia was not about smooth transitions; rather, it was about staying present with the jagged edges of life and death, and learning to sob unabashedly as needed whenever, wherever.

If you have ever been on a journey with someone going through chemotherapy, you know the roller-coaster ride. One day there is improvement; the next day brings a huge setback. It is a delicate alchemy to stop the growth of cancer without killing the patient in the process.

My father went to the doctor originally because he had persistent flu-like symptoms. He called me from the hospital to tell me the doctors had found leukemia in 80 percent of his blastic (new) blood cells. Had he waited another day or two without seeking treatment, he would have died.

I immediately packed my bags and flew to North Carolina to be with my dad, my mom, and my sister. I visited often over the next two years and spent as many days as I could at my father's side during his illness.

This second dance with death with someone very important to me was different from the first death waltz with don Miguel. I hated seeing my father in pain. I hated feeling helpless. I struggled with the pressing weight of unsaid words.

While I loved my father and I knew he loved me, we had a challenging relationship. He was a businessman with very high standards, and growing up I never felt like I was perfect enough for him. I went through phases of getting straight As and doing everything I could to please him, and then I would rebel, frustrated and feeling like he never really saw me. Our relationship had improved as I matured, but I still found myself getting triggered when he questioned what I was doing. There were times even as an adult when I still felt like a little girl seeking his approval. I often felt the unanswered questions that hung in the air between us: Am I good enough? Do you love me? Although I had done my best to clean up any unresolved area, the weight of the past still hung over our relationship.

I was in Scotland with a group of dear friends when I received a call that the leukemia within my father was back in force after a brief, three-month remission. But unlike with the call regarding Miguel when I was in Hawaii, this time I was overcome with debilitating grief and a feeling of incompleteness. I put the phone down and went for a walk through the heather and ferns on the hill behind the retreat center. With each step I sobbed, asking "Why, why, why?" I found a bench and crawled into a little ball, letting my tears baptize my face, my shirt, and the wooden backrest I was crying against. I felt my world was coming apart, and I had no control or say in the way things would unfold.

Writing this still brings tears to my eyes many years later. Now mixed in with the sadness is the joy of knowing my father: the man who saved me from the monkey pulling my hair when I was five, the man who came to every track meet, the man who taught me to keep going when the going got tough. But now, upon hearing that the end was imminent, the going now felt too tough, the road too steep. I walked back down the hill with my tears and snot and fractured spirit and sought out my friend and mentor, Peggy Dylan, for some advice.

"It just doesn't feel fair," I told her (something I used to regularly tell my dad when I was a kid. His reply was always, "Life isn't fair."). "I'm not ready for him to die. He is not ready to die. It just feels unfinished and not right. I want his death to be peaceful and for there to be a sense of completion," I said through my tears.

"This is an opportunity for you to love the jagged edges," Peggy said gently. "Life and death do not always bring us the timing or the situations we ask for. Can you stay present with the unfair, the unknown, the unfinished?"

And there it was, the answer that I wanted to bury my head in the sand to avoid. I was being asked to deepen my relationship with the Angel of Death. So I practiced loving and saying Yes to the jagged edges of my father's death. I did so by being present with him for his final late-night breaths, and supporting my mom and sister in their final good-byes to this man who had filled our lives.

I practiced staying with my own jagged edges, the internal shattering that happens when someone who is so much a part of your makeup dies. I gave myself permission to cry whenever I wanted to. I cried in public, at the movies (I once sat in the front row of an empty theater and cried through an entire teenager-from-the-rough-side-of-town-surprises-everyone-and-wins-the-prize dance movie), and at odd memories and unexpected reminders. I never questioned the tears; I just let them flow, let the grief take my breath away. The grief emptied me, polished my insides, made space for even more appreciation of the infinite blessings of every single in and out breath.

As a result of this experience with my father's passing, when I am called to sit at the bedside of someone dying, I am fully present, and I bring an open heart, softened by loss and strengthened by the knowing that the body is temporary but the spirit is eternal.

Noticing Our Attachments

When we enter the doorway of any intimate relationship, whether with a lifetime lover, a precious pet, a cherished child, or a favorite friend, our being expands in the delight of saying Yes! to love. We bond, we merge, we comingle, we grow familiar, but we also attach to our person or beloved. And, as Buddha said, attachment is the beginning of all suffering.

Combine a cup of unconscious attachment with a heaping scoop of impermanence and the end result is always the same: fear. This fear of loss causes us to grasp even more tightly to the object of our love and to fervently hold to the illusion that things will stay the same forever.

Of all the attachments we form in the world, the one that is the hardest to let go of is our association with the body. Because our body, everyone's body, eventually dies, yet the mind makes the association that we "are" our bodies. But when we look deeply into our hearts and listen to the wisdom we find there, we know that this isn't true. Our souls, our spirits, and our intent exist before and after they inhabit a particular body. We are timeless and eternal. Still, our attachment to the idea that we are our bodies is a persistent one, and the fear this attachment generates will cause suffering in our relationships if we don't examine it.

There is one truth for all relationships. No matter how long you are together, regardless of the vastness of your love for each other, despite the blessed wonderfulness of the relationship, eventually one body is going to leave the other. Either the nature of your relationship will shift, or you will get to experience the finality of "'til death do us part." No bodily relationship lasts forever, because no one gets out of here alive.

When you can see at depth that it's only the body that dies, physical death becomes not something you fear, but rather something to befriend, because it teaches you to embrace life with the fullness of your being. The same is true for change. When you understand that everything changes, the temporary nature of relationships grants you the opportunity to learn to love from your toenails to the tippy top of your head, and to let go of the object of your love at the same time.

The truth is that only one entity can take that luscious, divine love for another away from you, and that is not death, nor change, nor the other person. The only one who can do that is you. And you do this every time you judge, or place conditions, or hold resentments, and this is why we have spent so much time on the Warrior Goddess path learning how to release these traps that keep us from experiencing love.

Love becomes eternal when you remember that it is YOUR love, that you are the one doing the loving. The being on the receiving end may be sparking that torrent of love nectar bubbling out of your heart, but you are the source. Regardless of whether the objects of your love are breathing or not, with you or with another, when you are not attached to them you are freed up to do what is your nature: to love fully without fear of loss or abandonment. This is one of the most challenging lessons to practice on the Warrior Goddess path, and it takes great courage to walk down this road. Be gentle with yourself as you consider this.

How to Celebrate Death

The Mexican culture has a phenomenal relationship with death, and with life. Any occasion can bring on a fiesta complete with out-of-tune mariachis in tight pants and rhinestoned jackets, strangers welcomed as family, and lots of laughter. Everyone is always ready for a party. (When my friend Emily and her Mexican husband told his family that they would be getting married in two days, the family went into action: their wedding celebration was complete with a band, food, and a hundred people, all pulled together spur of the moment.)

Along with their love of celebrating life to the fullest, the Mexicans' relationship to the Angel of Death is known around the world. At the end of October, most of the country turns their eyes and hearts toward the Beloved Dead. This festival was originally an Aztec festival to the goddess of death, Mictecacihuatl, and was moved to coincide with the European festivals of Hallowmas (now known as Halloween) and All Saints' Day, when the Spanish invaded Mexico.

During Día de los Muertos, participants build elaborate altars for those who have died, visit graveyards and have picnics complete with foods that the dead loved, and sometimes have parades through villages carrying pictures of their beloved dead. There are pictures and statues everywhere of skeletons doing everyday things: a skeleton human walking a skeleton dog, a skeleton bride and groom, a skeleton kicking back and drinking a beer. It is a beautiful way to remind us that we are already dead, as none of us is getting out of here alive.

This tradition also blurs the hard and fast lines we sometime draw between the living and the dead. The truth is not so black and white. As soon as we are born, we start moving toward death. If we try to avoid that truth, we end up clinging to the past and fearing the future.

Some of my favorite words about death come from a speech Steve Jobs gave at Stanford after he had surgery for pancreatic cancer:

> No one wants to die. Even people who want to go to heaven don't want to die to get there. And yet death is the destination we all share. No one has ever escaped it. And that is as it should be, because death is very likely the single best invention of life.

It is life's change agent. It clears out the old to make way for the new. Right now the new is you, but someday not too long from now, you will gradually become the old and be cleared away.

So, my sweethearts, you don't have to like death (or endings), but I invite you to fall in love with it. I invite you to say Yes to it. Accepting and embracing death does not mean you will bring it toward you faster, or that you are a masochist. It means that you are honest with what being alive really means.

Embrace the fact that everything that is born ultimately dies. Don't avoid it, or run from it, or try to ignore it. Bring the Angel of Death in close, so she can remind you to not waste your life trying to be someone you are not. Use the knowledge of your death to follow your heart, to be courageous, to claim the woman you are destined to be.

When we say Yes to the blessed, bittersweet, mysterious partnership of the Angel of Life and the Angel of Death, we hold hands with both, walking arm in arm with both birth and death, day and night, beginnings and endings as equal partners. Turn and see yourself through the compassionate eyes of the Angel of Death so she can help you surrender that which is not yours. Say Yes to this fleeting, exquisite, humbling river of life that will lovingly strip you down to the freedom of your sacred bones.

Yes!: Death Resources

Gifts

- Befriending death frees you to be more fully engaged with life.

- We honor our humanity and the gifts of those we love when we open to grief and stay with the jagged edges of death.

- Learn to celebrate death, and let your gratitude for your ancestors and beloved dead grow your capacity to love deeply.

Explorations

REFLECTION ON DEATH

Find a quiet space where you can imagine death claiming your beloved. Sit comfortably and breathe into your heart.

Enter into this practice with curiosity and courage. What will arise? Be open to any emotions, thoughts, and old beliefs. Remember that this process is about cleaning out anything that lies between you and your freedom to love fearlessly.

Imagine your beloved is dead. With your witness hat on, let your emotions and thoughts bubble up into your conscious mind. Pay close attention to all the data that presents itself.

You can make it more real by imagining the method of their death and how you first hear the news. Imagine your days and nights without them. Make it as vivid as possible. (But don't traumatize yourself. Take it slowly, especially if huge emotions arise that take away your ability to witness.)

From this place of deep reflection, now ask yourself the following questions:

- Are there any ways I don't feel complete with this person?

- Do I have any regrets?

• What thoughts or beliefs are behind my emotions?

In doing this practice with beloveds and friends, I have noticed that sometimes I feel complete and bathed in my love for this precious human. Sometimes I think I cannot live without them. Sometimes I feel immense grief. Sometimes I realize something I want to share with them before they die. It's all good, and it points me in the direction of where I need to clean my internal world and clear up anything that is unresolved with them as best I can.

Regularly releasing your beloveds will help you to:

• Keep your slate clean of fear and regret.

• Use the gift of impermanence as a motivator to love more, not as an excuse to love less.

• Not slip into complacency or taking another for granted.

• Strengthen your relationships.

• Feel safe and confident in yourself.

• Root into what is eternal.

CREATING AN ALTAR TO YOUR BELOVED DEAD

On my four-drawer wooden filing cabinet in my office, I have an altar with a picture of my father holding me as a baby, a photo of him a year before he died, and his obituary. He is kept company by two of my students, David Ray and Zaneta Matkowska, who died several years ago. Now that I look at David's and Zaneta's photographs, I notice that in these particular pictures they are both sitting on boulders and grinning. They never knew each other, but each one's obvious love of nature and of life shines through in these images.

My death altar also has a small, beautiful wooden clock that stopped not long after I gave it to my dad on some Christmas passed, my grandfather's brown-beaded rosary, and a plastic faerie warrior princess complete with sword and wings in honor of Zaneta.

I invite you to build yourself an altar for anyone in your life who has died. Add some photos and some whimsy. Grieve and share your love. Cry buckets and laugh fully as needed.

THE ART OF SAYING GOOD-BYE

I create little rituals with myself to help me release the past and stay in the present. One is that every time I get on a plane I very mindfully look at the window and as the plane's wheels leave the earth I wave good-bye to everything I am leaving behind. "Bye-bye, Austin!" "Bye-bye, Mexico!" "Bye-bye, New York!" Then I send gratitude to all the things I am letting go: my house, my friends, a city I love. I know that this helps me travel as fluidly as I do.

When something leaves my life, from a relationship to a self-concept to my favorite shawl, I literally wave and say, "Bye-bye! I love you!" My close friends know the game, and sometimes when life shifts suddenly in front of us we'll both say, "bye-bye!" and then giggle, or hold hands and feel the loss.

Try consciously saying, "Bye-bye, I love you" to the things that disappear, dissolve, or die. When you move out of a house, say good-bye and share your gratitude. At your child's birthday or your own, wave good-bye to the previous age. "Bye-bye, and thanks for her thirteenth year!" "Bye-bye to forty-nine, and thank you!"

Say "bye-bye" to the sun when the clouds come, to the flowers that become withered and dry, to every day before you go to sleep. This practice will help you stay more open-hearted when the big good-byes come.

Afterword:
Homecoming and
Coming Home

Women are always at the front of revolutions.
—Buthayna Kamel

As a woman my country is the whole world.
—Virginia Woolf

Wisdom, Authenticity, Yes!

These are the treasures of the Warrior Goddess Way. This is the path of letting our wisdom, authenticity, and Yes! shine through us as we embrace our fears, our awkwardness, our inner beauty, and our sometimes crazy minds. This path leads to one place: ourselves. It is time for us to come home to ourselves, to cherish and celebrate the breadth and depth of ourselves: the goofy, serious, visionary, practical, silly, grounded Warrior Goddesses that we are.

At the same time as we are each coming home to ourselves, we are also part of a global homecoming, a collective return to the divine feminine. We are each part of an inner revolution *and* an outer paradigm shift that are intimately connected. We are *coming home* to ourselves and experiencing a *homecoming* to the divine feminine simultaneously.

For our ancestors, home was the earth, and the Goddess. She was the Mother Earth who nourished us, and her voice came through the wind and the mountains, and all humans and animals and plants were her children. Imagine a mother who loves you fiercely and unconditionally. A mother who holds you when you are scared and soothes you with her words and touch. A mother who looks you straight in the eye and says, "You can do this" when you are hesitant about trying something new. A mother who is always there when you need her, and encourages you to explore and fall down and get back up so you learn from experience. A mother who mirrors your wisdom, supports you in your authenticity, and wants you to live your life from an ecstatic Yes! This mother represents the spirit of the divine feminine, and she goes by many names: Goddess, Mother Earth, Divine Mother, Mary, Kuan Yin, Kali, and many, many more.

As we return home to our own hearts, it is also time to come back to the unconditional love and support of the Divine Mother. This coming home and homecoming are not separate, or sequential; they are the inhale and the exhale of our journey as individuals and as humanity. With each inhale we come home to ourselves and our Warrior Goddess within. With each exhale we connect with Divine Mother—a homecoming with our family, friends, the birds, and roses and rocks—and breathe the manifestations of her love back into us. I experienced a taste of this sacred homecoming myself recently that I'd like to share with you.

A Pilgrimage to the Heart

To finish *The Warrior Goddess Way* I spent three weeks in Mexico on retreat, surrounded by a culture that fervently loves the Mother. I stayed at my friends Emily and Victor's house, which is filled with paintings and statues honoring the divine feminine, most of them depicting Our Lady of Guadalupe.

Also known as the Virgin of Guadalupe, this manifestation of the Divine Mother appeared to Juan Diego in 1531 and asked that he deliver a message to the bishop: build me a temple. It took some convincing, but when Juan Diego opened his cloak to reveal an image of Our Lady, the bishop knelt in reverence, and soon the temple construction was under way.

In his comprehensive book *The Aztec Virgin,* John Mini writes that the true name of Our Lady of Guadalupe, first spoken in Nahuatl (and then misinterpreted) is Tecuauhtlacuepeuh, "she who comes flying from the region of light like an eagle of fire." That sounds like a serious Warrior Goddess to me. She is the embodiment of the ancient Goddess of Mexico, Coatlicue, or Tonāntzin.

I felt strongly called to come to Teotihuacan on retreat during this time, and despite not completely understanding why, I listened to my heart and I came. My mind came up with lots of logical reasons to do so: finish the book, practice my Spanish, enjoy the holidays, etc. But then I saw a poster that made me laugh out loud—because I realized why I had felt such a strong inner pull to come: it was the Divine Mother herself who had called me here. The large, handwritten, black marker on yellow poster board invited anyone in the village to join in the pilgrimage to the Basilica of Our Lady of Guadalupe in Mexico City. December 11 is the day millions of people pilgrimage from all over the country.

The Mother was calling me home, again.

So in the midst of writing *The Warrior Goddess Way,* I walked forty-five miles from the pyramids at Teotihuacan to Tepeyac Hill in Mexico City, arriving just before midnight, each step a homecoming where I took each of you with me, step after step.

You see, I dedicated this pilgrimage to our collective homecoming to the Divine Mother. As I walked, I carried around two hundred prayers sent from Warrior Goddesses all over the world: Pray for my family. Pray for my children. Pray for North Korea. Pray for the people of South Africa. Pray for humanity. I said these blessings over and over again. I sang to the Goddess in her many forms: Isis, Astarte, Diana, Hecate, Demeter, Kali. I held my mala and chanted "Om Shanti." I offered these prayers over and over throughout the ten hours I walked from the pyramids to the basilica.

For the first three hours the group I was with walked along the railroad tracks toward Mexico City. Sometimes on the small dirt paths beside the tracks, sometimes on roads through little towns, sometimes walking the rocky path between the endless metal rails when there was no other option. A rancher on his horse shouted his blessings to us. Shepherds nodded as we passed by. We walked through unplowed fields, between cactus and brush, under freeways. At times villagers on their way to school or the grocery store briefly walked with us.

And then we turned left and headed into the city. Once we reached the edge of Mexico City, after three hours or so of being one distinct group, we merged with and then passed another group of *peregrinos* (pilgrims) dressed in neon green shirts with the image of Guadalupe. As our two groups mixed, I had a vision of the millions of people all across Mexico at that moment, all walking toward the heart of the Mother. We were individual cells coming back home to be replenished, oxygenated, loved, and sent back out again. The tiny venules at the extremities merged into larger ones as we got closer. As we edged closer and closer to the Basilica of Our Lady of

Guadalupe, our group was engulfed by hundreds of other peregrinos, and then the hundreds became thousands.

I was also touched by the staggering number of people standing like rocks in the midst of the flow, all there to support our journey. They passed out bottles of water, steaming tamales, juice, ham and cheese sandwiches, oranges, coffee, and an abundance of candy. Here was mutual service in action: we were walking to Guadalupe not just for ourselves but for everyone, and we were being blessed and supported all along the way.

As it grew dark, and our walking pace slowed due to the sheer number of people in the procession, I suddenly felt my heart connect to Tepeyac, the mountain where Guadalupe first introduced herself to Juan Diego. I felt the spirit of the mountain deep within me, and my heart flowered into a profound silence and peace. The noise of Mexico surrounded me on all sides, but the dark, silent sweetness of Tepeyac inside of me was a galaxy.

As I approached the final steps to the basilica, the prayers I had been chanting along the way simplified into an offering of gratitude: "*Gracias a mi madre. Gracias a mi madre. Gracias a mi madre.*" Standing in front of the main church, I knew it was time to let go of the group I had traveled there with and follow the pull I was feeling. I plunged into the unknown, letting go of my identification with my little tribe, and became part of the whole of humanity. I felt untethered, free, empty. I let the ocean of people and spirit and movement carry me.

I found myself in front of a group of Sufis, the mystical branch of the religion of Islam that is affectionately known as the whirling dervishes, given their propensity to ecstatic dancing. To some they might seem out of place, Muslims at a Christian ceremony, decorated with their tall felt hats and white flowing cotton dresses, but to me they fit perfectly. I inched closer and closer until I was in the outer circle of ecstasy. Music, movement, prayer, song going round and round. I merged with this group as they spun prayers and flung them into the sky. I cast the prayers I had been carrying into the middle of this vortex of love.

After releasing my prayers to the Divine Mother at the hands of these Sufis, I knew my pilgrimage was complete. I walked without thought back to my group, said good-bye, and then walked by myself to my hotel off Calzada de Guadalupe. It was incredible to be walking in Mexico City as a single female, at midnight, surrounded by people, totally safe and held in the arms of the Mother.

The next morning I went back up the avenue to the basilica to revel in the sacred jumble of people, cultures, and prayer. Fifty or so separate Aztec groups were scattered in the huge main plaza surrounded by churches, where they burned copal, prayed to the four directions, the old gods, and to Guadalupe, drumming and dancing and rattling, feathers and colors and bare skin. Inside the main cathedral mass was stoically proceeding, complete with a huge choir in red-and-white pressed gowns and much formality on the stage.

Everywhere, people carried statues and pictures of Our Lady of Guadalupe. Three million people came to the basilica that day to be blessed by Our Lady of Guadalupe, and seven million throughout the week. People laughed, wept, and prayed openly to the Divine Mother. The basilica was like a creative mash-up of a Grateful Dead show, Disneyland, church, and a pagan full moon ceremony all rolled into one. It was glorious, humbling, messy, and filled with love. After reflecting on the montage of beauty in front of me, I walked up to my favorite little church near the top of Tepeyac, sat down on the floor, and let the love I felt pour through me, and out to you.

This pilgrimage was another example of what I already knew to be true: this homecoming is happening now, just as the coming home we are all experiencing inside ourselves is happening now. The universe is a friendly place. Millions of us are ready to choose love over hate, to choose freedom instead of fear. When we come together, we have the power to release the old ways that have clouded our vision for so long.

Imagine that all of the ancestors are cheering you on, asking you to release your fears and bring forward the ancient wisdom of connection. Feel how you are surrounded by a global community of warriors of authenticity and goddesses of awareness. Vision that the unborn children and their children's children are saying to you: Yes! Embrace your strength. Yes! Claim your gifts. Yes! Own your uniqueness.

You are the ancestors and the unborn, the vibrant living and the beloved dead, the maiden and the crone. And your destiny awaits, hand stretched out, palm open, beckoning. Close your eyes, take the hand, and trust.

The Great Mother is waiting for you, and she is you, simultaneously. May we dissolve the illusion of separation, remember we are all cells in the body of the Great Mother, and surrender to being drawn back into Her heart and out again, to become Her heart in physical form. This is my prayer for you and for all beings.

And know that we are all together in spirit as we walk the Warrior Goddess Way.

Acknowledgments

Along with every single person named in my acknowledgments in *Warrior Goddess Training* (Thank you, thank you, thank you, again and again!!!), I also want to give my deepest gratitude to the following people who nourished and inspired me with their abounding friendship as I wrote *The Warrior Goddess Way*:

Kevin Braheny Fortune: blessings upon blessings for hammocks, radical honesty, and lifetimes of healing. I love you so.

Emily Grieves, your sisterhood and support and shared love of the Mother fill my heart to bursting.

Matthew Stillman, a deep bow for being a bridge and a catalyst in my life and for your superpowers with books and unanswerable questions.

Makenna Johnston, I so love growing our friendship and being lit up by your smile and sparkle and sass.

Perdita Finn and Clark Strand, thank you for your friendship, your writings, and your hearts, and for growing the soul-invigorating garden of the Way of the Rose. I'm honored to be one of the many roses you tend so generously.

And finally, to the expanding Warrior Goddess tribe, facilitators, and teachers, keep rocking your Warrior Goddess selves! Thank you for all you have done and continue to do.

Further Resources

Visit the Warrior Goddess website and get additional resources, including a list of local book clubs and facilitators at www.warriorgoddess.com.

Look for the *Warrior Goddess Way* book link on the front page and use the password "WGTBR" to get access to bonus material.

Like the Warrior Goddess Facebook page and get daily inspiration at www.facebook.com/warriorgoddesswomen. And circle up with the Warrior Goddess Tribe at www.facebook.com/warriorgoddesstribe.

Join a Warrior Goddess Training global circle via the Web or phone, or come to a Warrior Goddess Weekend or power journey. For more information, visit www.heatherashamara.com.

About the Author

HeatherAsh Amara is the author of *Warrior Goddess Training*, *Warrior Goddess Training Companion Workbook*, and *The Toltec Path of Transformation*. She is dedicated to inspiring depth, creativity, and joy by sharing the most potent tools from a variety of world traditions. HeatherAsh studied and taught extensively with don Miguel Ruiz, author of *The Four Agreements*, and continues to teach with the Ruiz family.

Raised in Southeast Asia, HeatherAsh has traveled the world and is continually inspired by the diversity and beauty of human expression and experience. She brings this open-hearted, inclusive worldview to her writings and teachings, which are a rich blend of Toltec wisdom, European shamanism, Buddhism, and Native American ceremony. Visit her online at www.heatherashamara.com.

Hierophant Publishing
8301 Broadway, Suite 219
San Antonio, TX 78209
888-800-4240

www.hierophantpublishing.com